Becoming a
TRUE
WORSHIPER

TOM KRAEUTER

P.O. BOX 635, LYNNWOOD, WA 98046

Emerald Books are distributed through YWAM Publishing. For a full list of titles, visit our website at www.ywampublishing.com or call 1-800-922-2143.

Becoming a True Worshiper
Copyright © 2006 by Training Resources, Inc.
8929 Old LeMay Ferry Road
Hillsboro, MO 63050
(636) 789-4522
www.training-resources.org

Published by Emerald Books
P.O. Box 635
Lynnwood, WA 98046

10 09 08 07 06   10 9 8 7 6 5 4 3 2 1

ISBN 1-932096-38-8

Library of Congress Cataloging-in-Publication Data
Kraeuter, Tom, 1958–
    Becoming a true worshiper / by Tom Kraeuter.
        p. cm.
    Includes bibliographical references.
    ISBN-13: 978-1-932096-38-5
    ISBN-10: 1-932096-38-8
    1. Worship—Biblical teaching. I. Title.
    BS680.W78K73 2006
    248.3'2—dc22   2006017921

Printed in the United States of America

I humbly dedicate this book to my dear friends the Petersen family—LeRoy and Marcia and their children, Carlee (Ragains), Shannon (Peters), Justin, Lucas, Josh, and Renée. You folks have been my friends and fellow sojourners in so many ways on the path of life. Thank you for your kindness, hospitality, prayers, and consistent example of Christ's love.

SPECIAL THANKS TO...

Jennifer Brody and Marit Newton for great editing work.

The thousands of worshipers who have attended our worship seminars and heard bits and pieces of this material formulate in my mind and heart.

Emerald Books for having enough confidence in my writing to publish yet another book by me.

And special thanks to my wife, Barbara, and our children, David, Stephen, and Amy, for loving me and allowing me the time to complete this manuscript.

CONTENTS

INTRODUCTION

Not long ago a friend of mine asked me, "Are you more interested in leading people in worship or in developing people into becoming worshipers?" I had never really considered this question before. As soon as the question was asked, though, I knew the "correct" answer.

As a worship leader, I have always been very interested in leading people in worship. However, it has become quite obvious to me that the higher priority is to develop people into *being* worshipers. That's my goal in writing this book: to help you become a true worshiper of God.

To that end we will first look at worship from a biblical perspective rather than from a cultural point of view, or even a traditional one. After that foundation has been laid, we will consider other practical steps on the road to becoming a true worshiper of God. I look forward to taking this journey with you.

As we begin, I would like to ask you a favor. Open your mind to what God has for you. He will transform you by renewing your mind as you look at the principles from His Word about worship. Set aside your preconceived ideas about worship, and join me in exploring from a biblical perspective what it means to be a true worshiper of God.

Though our thinking is often jolted and jarred whenever we truly delve into Scripture, I think you will find the final result worth the effort. In a magazine article, author Tricia McCary Rhodes said, "Two things ring true for me as I look over the landscape of my life as a worshiper: that it has cost far more than I ever dreamed, and that I have gained something far greater than I ever imagined."[1] I would definitely echo her statement. Truly being a worshiper is costly in both time and commitment, but the final result is worth far more than the effort. Always.

My prayer is that this book will help us to become the true worshipers that the Lord wants us to be.

chapter one

UNDERSTANDING WORSHIP

Years ago a series of black-and-white comedy movies were filmed featuring a group of silly, would-be thugs known as the Bowery Boys. More than forty Bowery Boys movies were filmed before I was born. Consequently, I am not overly familiar with all the characters. The main character, though, was very memorable. Slip Mahoney was malapropism[1] personified. He consistently used words that he clearly did not understand. Mahoney thought he understood, and most of the time the words he used sounded like the words he really should have been using. The results were often hilarious.

When I was younger, I had a friend who consistently said "re*numer*ation" when he meant "re*muner*ation." "Remuneration" means compensation or payment. "Renumeration" (not actually a word), on the other hand, could presumably mean to renumber something. It was almost the right word, but not quite.

Have you ever heard someone use a word incorrectly? The person may sound as though he or she is quite sure of him or herself, but the incorrect usage betrays the truth.

Many people in the church today say the word *worship* as though they are well acquainted with the term. Yet the context of their statement often betrays the fact that they really do not understand the word.

Not long ago Christian pollster George Barna surveyed people all across North America. Responding to the poll was not for just anyone, however. Barna talked only with those who regularly attend Christian churches. Keep this in mind. This survey was not for those who never grace a church with their presence. It was not even aimed at the poinsettia and lily crowd, the folks who go to church on Christmas and Easter. Those who responded to the poll were *regular attenders* of Christian churches.

Here's the reason I'm telling you this: Barna asked the survey takers to define *worship*. The poll results were stunning. Two out of three people either had no idea at all or offered a vague definition with no real meaning.

When I first heard these polling results, I was shocked. Why? Well, it seems to me that if someone is regularly involved in an activity—any activity—describing it, at least on some level, shouldn't be terribly difficult. If you regularly play golf, wash windows, grill hamburgers, sew on buttons, or lay carpet, most likely you can offer some sort of description of those activities—*What is it you do?*—to someone. If people are actually involved in worship on a regular basis, the majority ought to be able to offer a credible answer as to what it is.

Unfortunately, Barna's survey clearly shows that two-thirds of those who regularly attend Christian churches in North America do not really know what worship is. If you include those who go to church only occasionally, the percentage is even higher. The conclusion is sadly clear. The overwhelming majority of those in North American Christian churches on Sunday mornings do not honestly understand the concept of worship.

At this point you may be wondering, "What's the big deal? So what if they can't explain worship?" Apparently from God's perspective it is a big deal. Worship is not just a suggestion in the Bible. We are repeatedly *commanded* to worship God.

> Ascribe to the LORD the glory due his name; *worship the LORD*. (Psalm 29:2)

> *Worship the LORD* in the splendor of holiness. (Psalm 96:9)

> "*You shall worship the Lord your God* and him only shall you serve." (Matthew 4:10)

And those are just a few references. You and I both know that over and over again throughout the pages of Scripture we are commanded to worship the Lord.

So, if most people who attend church week after week don't really know what worship is and yet God's Word commands us to do it, the question that must be answered is, What is worship? Socrates said, "Before anyone can intelligently discuss a subject, one must first define the term." For us as Christians, it is imperative that we define worship from a biblical perspective. Unless we use God's Word to arrive at an understanding, we have no real basis for a definition. You see, we can call something anything we want to, but that does not mean the thing really is what we've called it.

After a lengthy speech by his political opponent, Abraham Lincoln reportedly asked the audience, "How many legs would a horse have if you called his tail a leg?" When some in the crowd answered, "Five," Lincoln responded, "No, just four. Calling a tail a leg doesn't make it a leg."

In the same way, simply calling something worship does not necessarily make it worship. We must look at it from a biblical viewpoint. W. Nicholls said it this way:

> Worship is the supreme and only indispensable activity of the Christian church. It alone will endure, like the love for God which it expresses, into heaven, when all other activities of the Church will have passed away. It must therefore, even more strictly than any of the less essential doings of the Church, come under the criticism and control of the revelation on which the Church is founded.[2]

In other words, even more than the peripheral issues of the Christian life, worship—of primary importance— must be biblical.

When I was in seminary, one of the professors gave a rather involved assignment: do a word study on the word *worship*. We were to find all the times in our English translations of the Bible where the word *worship* is used. By looking at the original languages—Hebrew and Greek—we were then to see what the words that we translated as *worship* literally meant. We were told to come to some overall conclusions about worship based on this study.

If you do a study like this, and you do it honestly, you will come to at least three very clear and extremely obvious conclusions about worship:

1. Worship honors God.
2. Worship is directed toward God.
3. Worship requires involvement on the part of the worshiper.

Actually, it is not even necessary to look at the original languages to see this. Even a cursory look at worship in the Bible will show this concept to be true. Here are some examples:

All Judah and the inhabitants of Jerusalem fell down before the LORD, worshiping the LORD. (2 Chronicles 20:18)

And they bowed their heads and worshiped the LORD with their faces to the ground. (Nehemiah 8:6)

And they came up and took hold of [Jesus'] feet and worshiped him. (Matthew 28:9)

Present your bodies as a living sacrifice, holy and acceptable to God, which is your spiritual worship. (Romans 12:1)

The twenty-four elders fall down before him who is seated on the throne and worship him who lives forever and ever. (Revelation 4:10)

In each of these (and so many other) passages of Scripture, as the people worship, they are *honoring* God, their worship is directed *toward* God, and there is an obvious *involvement* on the part of the worshiper. Let's take a brief look at each of these three aspects independently.

Worship Honors God

A fundamental understanding of worship is that it must honor God. One of the most apparent places to see this is from the origin of the English word *worship*. In his book *Understanding Music & Worship in the Local Church*, Vernon M. Whaley explained it this way: "The word worship comes from the Anglo-Saxon weorthscipe which meant to 'ascribe worth, to pay homage, to reverence or venerate.' The word was modified to worthship and then to what we use today, worship. What a person values (or places a high worth upon) is what will be worshiped."[3]

The word *worthship* was often used to address or describe someone of importance, someone worthy of honor or respect. In fact, even after it was shortened to worship, in some circles the word is still used this same way today. If you were to visit Great Britain and you were introduced to a dignitary in a certain town, he might be introduced as "His Worship, the Mayor of _____." This would mean not that the mayor is to be worshiped as we might think of this word from a Christian perspective, but that he is worthy of honor and respect. It is a term to show honor to someone.

In the context of our faith it takes on an even higher understanding. Who is more worthy of honor than God? No one. He is the one who is to be supremely worshiped!

Worship, then, is not primarily for our benefit. Later in this book we will discuss the fact that we will profit from worshiping God, but that is not the main focus of worship. Our worship is to honor God.

Some time ago my pastor said it this way: "We act as if the worship service were supposed to be a production done in 'Our Royal Honor.' But that's as far from biblical worship as heaven is from earth."[4] He's right. Worship is not about us. To be called true worship, it must honor God.

Not long ago I read an article on an interesting Web site, www.iplasma.com. The article was entitled, "Worship? Churches Are So Out of Focus." The writer shared these poignant thoughts:

> One of the attributes of biblical worship is its primary focus on God. "Primary focus" because, in reality, a God-orientation (i.e., a concentration on Creator, Redeemer, and Sustainer) will naturally come back to embrace who we are as humans: the created, redeemed, and sustained.... However, it has become entirely possible to forego the God-orientation entirely. Instead of a vertical relationship between worshiper and The One Worshiped, these kinds of services are essentially flattened to a congregation's experience of themselves. Translated, "It's about us."

While visiting a church several years ago, I heard the pastor tell this provocative story. All the bridesmaids have just walked slowly down the aisle. The organ bursts forth with the first strains of the Wedding March, and the back door of the church opens wide. The bride appears.

There is a collective gasp at her breathtaking beauty. All over the building murmurings of "Isn't she beautiful?" and "My, how lovely!" can be heard. Most of these comments are too soft and too far away for her to hear, but several are within her earshot. Suddenly she begins to realize how absolutely gorgeous she really is. Immediately one hand goes on her hip and she strikes a pose for the photographer. She then drops her bouquet and puts her other hand behind her head giving the camera buffs another great shot of her beauty. As this continues the crowd turns toward the groom. The comments of "Isn't she beautiful?" have now changed to "Oh the poor man. She loves herself more than she loves him."

What an unthinkable scenario. However, this just may be a fairly accurate portrayal of the state of Christianity in America. It's all about us. True worship, on the other hand, is all about honoring God.

In his book *For All God's Worth*, N. T. Wright offers some thoughts on the proper orientation of worship:

> Worship is humble and glad; worship forgets itself in remembering God; worship celebrates the truth as God's truth, not its own. True worship doesn't put on a show or make a fuss; true worship isn't forced, isn't halfhearted, doesn't keep looking at its watch, doesn't worry what the person in the next pew may be doing. True worship is open to God, adoring God, waiting for God, trusting God.[5]

True worship will reorient our thinking. It takes our eyes off self and circumstances and focuses us toward honoring God.

Worship Is Directed Toward God

Truly biblical worship is not just a time during which we talk *about* God. Our words and actions must be directed *toward* Him. One of my favorite authors, Jerry Bridges, has written numerous books. One that I read just a couple of years ago was entitled *The Joy of Fearing God*. In it, Bridges made this statement:

> It isn't my intent to make a judgment statement about any church service that emphasizes evangelism or body life or teaching. I do believe that such a service should not be called a *worship* service. A worship service should focus on God. This doesn't mean that ministry to members of the body or even to unbelievers will not occur. It does mean that the emphasis is on worship of God, ascribing to Him the praise, adoration, and thanksgiving that are due Him.[6]

Again and again when we see worship happening in the pages of Scripture, the object of the worship is the Lord. The word *worship* is not used to talk about God but rather is directed toward Him.

Some years ago I attended a Christian conference. A man who spoke during one of the general sessions mentioned that he had been in another city on business over a weekend. He was there with a friend, and since both were followers of Christ, on Sunday morning they went to a local gathering of believers. As they left the service, the friend seemed a bit frustrated. He turned to the man and said, "I really enjoyed the sermon there this morning, but I didn't get much out of the worship."

The man looked at his friend and asked, "Have you ever considered what that has to do with anything?" In essence, he was asking, "Whom is the worship for?" Worship is not for us. It is the creature honoring the Creator. It is the redeemed loving and adoring the Redeemer. It is not for us; it is for God. Worship must be directed toward Him.

Recently my family and I visited a church in another part of the country. We were in the area for an athletic competition in which our son was participating, and this church was a convenient place for our Sunday-morning worship. Before the service I looked through the church bulletin. Besides the "Special Music" and the response song after the sermon, two other song segments, with two songs listed for each, were planned. The two main times during which the congregation would be called on to sing were "Songs of Worship" and "Fellowship Songs." The two songs listed under "Songs of Worship" were "Think About His Love" and "What a Friend We Have in Jesus." Lyrically, both of these "songs of worship" are sung to one another. We were certainly not telling God to "think about His love." We were singing words that were written to be sung to one another, yet the bulletin labeled this "Songs of *Worship*."

I thought that was rather strange, but later the service took an even stranger turn. When we got to the "Fellowship Songs," the two songs listed were "Ancient of Days" and "As the Deer." Try to picture this scenario. We walked about greeting one another with the words "Every tongue in heaven and earth shall declare *Your* glory" and "I long to worship *You*." Huh?! We're singing songs *to* God, and these were referred to as "Fellowship Songs"? I thought, *It is no wonder most people have difficulty describing worship. If church leadership can't get it right, how can we expect the folks in the pews to understand?*

Let me offer a brief grammar lesson that may prove helpful. Worship is a transitive verb. It needs an object. My friend Bob Kauflin likens it to the word *throw.* You can't throw nothing. There must be something to throw in order to use the word *throw.* Throw...what? Throw a baseball? Throw a party? The word needs an object. In the same way, worship needs an object. Worship...what (or who)? Worship the Lord!

To truly be called *worship* it must be directed toward God.

Worship Requires Involvement on the Part of the Worshiper

Whenever we see worship occurring in the pages of Scripture, people are *doing* something. They are not casually observing but are actively participating.

Yes, I know there is one time in the Bible when Jacob leaned on his staff and worshiped (Genesis 47:31). That, however, is the exception! The overwhelming majority of times Scripture talks of bowing and singing and speaking forth words of praise and clapping and shouting and giving and kneeling and raising hands—a number of participatory actions to worship the Lord. Clearly these kinds of activities require involvement on the part of the worshiper.

Part of the dilemma we face in our society is that as a culture we have adopted the Greek theory of man that separates the mind from the body. The Jewish understanding, which is much more biblical, is holistic: the mind and body work together. Of course, we should recognize that the mind and the body perform different functions. However, viewing them as part of a whole instead of separate entities changes our perspective on how we worship.

When I see myself as one whole being (instead of separate mind and body entities), I cannot possibly have the attitude, "I know I am sitting here looking very staid, but inside I'm shouting about the majesty of God." If you truly see yourself as a complete person, not just compartmentalized sections, you can never honestly think, "I may be standing here looking unfazed, but inside I am prostrated before the holy, sovereign God of the universe!" A truly biblical perspective says, "I am one whole person, and therefore my worship must involve my whole being."

If we are to be honest in our worship—not pretending—we must be truthful throughout our whole being. Merely thinking nice thoughts toward the Lord is to ignore part of who we are. There is an involvement that is necessary in our worship.

James makes a clear case for this. "Show me your faith apart from your works, and I will show you my faith by my works.... Faith apart from works is dead" (James 2:18, 26). James is telling us that what is on the inside needs to be demonstrated on the outside. Our faith and the subsequent expressions of our faith cannot be simply internalized. They must make it to the outside.

Prior to the Reformation, the worship of the Church was slowly but surely transferred from the people to the clergy. The congregation had become an audience. It watched and listened to the "worship" but had very little real involvement in it. Worship became something that was done to the people rather than something the people did. One of the main thrusts of the reformers was to return worship to the people. It was during the Reformation that the phrase "priesthood of all believers" (based on 1 Peter 2:5, 9; Revelation 1:6; 5:10; 20:6) was coined. Worship is not to be a spectator sport. Worship requires involvement.

Dr. Robert Webber has been considered by many in the North American church as "Mr. Worship." He has written numerous books and taught numerous seminars on the subject. Dr. Webber was the theological editor for the *Praise and Worship Study Bible* from Tyndale and even compiled a monumental eight-volume encyclopedia on worship. One of his book titles, now more than two decades old, sums up my point here: *Worship Is a Verb.* It's true. There is an involvement that is necessary in true, biblical worship.

Too frequently today people try to take the word *worship* and analyze it, examining it from every conceivable angle, just as they would a diamond or a new puppy. But worship is not a thing to be observed, inspected, and scrutinized. It is something to be done. It is not an object but an activity. As such, worship requires involvement.

New Testament Worship

Before we conclude this section, it is necessary to mention that a fourth aspect of worship is peculiarly a New Testament concept. It is an aspect that is absolutely essential to our understanding of Christian worship. Apart from Jesus' atoning sacrifice, our most noble and heart-felt acts of worship are not acceptable to God. Scripture says, "*Through [Jesus] then let us continually offer up a sacrifice of praise to God, that is, the fruit of lips that acknowledge his name*" (Hebrews 13:15). It is only because of the death and resurrection of Christ that we can even approach God to worship Him.

Peter the apostle said it similarly. "You yourselves like living stones are being built up as a spiritual house, to be a holy priesthood, to offer spiritual sacrifices *acceptable to God through Jesus Christ*" (1 Peter 2:5). It is only through Christ's sacrifice on the cross that even our praises are made acceptable to the Lord. Without Him and what He has done, we have nothing.

When Paul writes to the saints at Rome, he says, "I appeal to you therefore, brothers, *by the mercies of God*, to present your bodies as a living sacrifice, holy and acceptable to God, which is your spiritual worship" (Romans 12:1). Paul says that we should give ourselves to the Lord because of the mercies of God. Only because of what Jesus did on the cross—the mercies of God made manifest—can we willingly present ourselves to the Lord.

Yes, I recognize that I am implying exclusivity here. I am doing so because Jesus Himself did. "No one comes to the Father except through me" (John 14:6). That is clearly an exclusive statement. True worship has restrictions. It cannot include an ecumenical ideology that embraces all people, regardless of their religious affiliation, as one. Without Jesus' death on the cross and His subsequent resurrection, we have absolutely no right to come before God. On the other hand, in light of His atoning work—and only because of that work—we have every right to approach the King.

At this point I hope we have adopted a much clearer understanding of worship than we had when we began. Worship

- ◆   honors God;
- ◆   is directed toward God;

- requires involvement on the part of the worshiper;
- is available only through Jesus Christ.

At this point you and I would be better prepared for the Barna poll mentioned earlier. Of course, the goal of this book is not so much to prepare us for responding to a survey but to help us recognize and experience true worship. Since the chapters to come contain plenty more for us to discover about God's perspective on worship, let's now move on.

chapter two

WORSHIPING IN
SPIRIT AND TRUTH

You are probably familiar with the story of Jesus talking to the Samaritan woman at the well. During the conversation, Jesus pinpoints some areas of her life that He could not have known about in the natural. As a result, the woman declares Him to be a prophet.

> The woman said to him, "Sir, I perceive that you are a prophet. Our fathers worshiped on this mountain, but you say that in Jerusalem is the place where people ought to worship."
> Jesus said to her, "Woman, believe me, the hour is coming when neither on this mountain nor in Jerusalem will you worship the Father. You worship what you do not know; we worship what we know, for salvation is from the Jews. But the hour is coming,

and is now here, when the true worshipers will worship the Father in spirit and truth, for the Father is seeking such people to worship him. God is spirit, and those who worship him must worship in spirit and truth." (John 4:19–24)

In this section of Scripture, Jesus has clearly expressed a preference for the Jewish worship rather than the Samaritan worship. He says, "You worship what you do not know; we worship what we know, for salvation is from the Jews." Yet after He makes that statement, He goes on to suggest the imperfection of even the Jewish worship when He comments, "But the hour is coming…" Though the Jewish worship was better than the Samaritan worship, it was still not perfect.

In honestly evaluating Jesus' words here, it seems fair to say that it is possible for us to have a better form of worship than someone else's and yet still not worship exactly as God wants us to. Stated another way, the corporate worship of your church may be better than that of the church down the road but still not be quite what the Lord is looking for. If this is true, the real question becomes, What is it that God wants?

Jesus said that true worshipers "must worship in spirit and truth." In this chapter we'll explore both of these, starting with what it means to worship in spirit.

Worshiping in Spirit

To understand what Jesus was driving at, it is first essential to have a brief lesson in language. In any language—your native tongue or any other—certain words can be used interchangeably. Seemingly all languages have words that are synonymous, words that can be exchanged for one another. For example, I could say, "My family and I have a vehicle that we drive. It is a car. It has proven to be a very dependable automobile." Those three sentences contain three words, "vehicle," "car," and "automobile," that could be moved around—interchanged—and still maintain the meaning. All languages contain certain words that mean pretty much the same and can be substituted for one another.

According to *Vine's Expository Dictionary of Biblical Words*, a few different definitions of the word *spirit* are used in this passage from John's Gospel. However, the one that has the most biblical support is "the sentient element in man, that by which he perceives, reflects, feels, desires." In essence, it is the inner us. We could clearly liken it to the biblical understanding of *heart*. It's a different word, but the same meaning. In the biblical context, *heart* and *spirit* are basically synonymous.

To worship in spirit, then, means to engage the inner self. True worship means not just going through the motions but responding to God with an honest heart. The Lord makes this clear in a poignant passage from the book of Isaiah:

> "Hear the word of the LORD, you rulers of Sodom! Give ear to the teaching of our God, you people of Gomorrah!" (Isaiah 1:10)

Before we go too far here, let me interject that God is not speaking to Sodom and Gomorrah in these verses. He is addressing His chosen people, Israel, but He is not very happy with them. He has resorted to calling them names!

"What to me is the multitude of your sacrifices?" says the LORD; "I have had enough of burnt offerings of rams and the fat of well-fed beasts; I do not delight in the blood of bulls, or of lambs, or of goats. When you come to appear before me, who has required of you this trampling of my courts? Bring no more vain offerings; incense is an abomination to me. New moon and Sabbath and the calling of convocations— I cannot endure iniquity and solemn assembly. Your new moons and your appointed feasts my soul hates; they have become a burden to me; I am weary of bearing them." (Isaiah 1:11–14)

Several years ago I read this section of Scripture. I stopped at the end of verse 14 and thought, *Hold on a minute! Who was it who had asked for all these things?* Who had requested the feasts, the incense, the offerings, and the sacrifices? Who was it? It was God.

The Lord Himself had specifically asked for each of these, and here He is denouncing them. Why? After all, the people were doing the things He had told them to do, and yet God is upbraiding them for it. This seems wrong. Why on earth would the Lord chastise His people for doing the very things He told them to do? What's going on here?

At this point in Israel's history I cannot imagine it was because the people were doing the activities incorrectly. In fact, by this time the people of Israel were probably so good at any or all of them that they could do them without even thinking about them. That, it appears, was the problem. They were going through the motions but without the inner self. The people of Israel were doing everything the Lord had told them to do—crossing each *t*, dotting every *i*—but without engaging the heart and spirit. They got the outside right but missed the all-important inside. And the Lord said, "Not interested."

One of the main messages of the Old Testament prophets was their condemnation of the Israelite worship because it had become only an outward ritual with no heart. The Hebrews were doing all the outward forms that God had instructed. Unfortunately, they were ignoring the spirit of what they were doing.

Actually, we can be just as guilty today. Let me be extremely candid for a moment. I have even been *leading* worship and done the same thing. There have been times when I have stood in front of a congregation of people, leading them in songs filled with words of heartfelt adoration while thinking, "Let's see…this afternoon I need to mow the lawn…." I hope that you can't relate to that, but I fear that you can.

We are creatures of habit. It is all too easy for us to go through the motions and miss the meaning. Part of this is because we do the same thing over and over. After a while, we get the hang of it and go through the routine without thinking about it. In some instances this can be quite helpful. I'm very glad, for example, that I do not need to relearn how to drive a car each time I get into one. I've been at it long enough now that I can pretty well do it without thinking about it. This can also be a bad thing. The other day I got a ticket for driving too fast. My mind was somewhere else, and I pushed too hard on the accelerator. I was going through the routine, but my inner self was absent.

Similarly, routine can be—is not necessarily, but can be—the enemy of true heartfelt worship. Suppose I have an unchanging routine I go through each day in my relationship with my wife. If, out of rote, I simply repeat the same phrases and perform the same actions, they can easily lose significance. Every morning I could go through a carefully planned checklist to be certain I have not missed anything. After meticulously checking my list, each day I would call out to my wife, "Honey, I love you." Then I would think, *There, I took care of that one.* I could check it off the list and then think, *Now, on to the next item on the list.* This could easily become an external ritual with no reality for me. The same can happen in worship.

You are probably familiar with the Christian tradition of people making the sign of the cross. First they touch the forehead and then move the hand down to the chest and then side to side. Do you know the original meaning of that action? The symbolism is actually very powerful. Someone making the sign of cross is saying, "I love the Lord with my whole mind" (touching the forehead). "I love the Lord with my whole heart" (touching the chest). "I love the Lord with my whole being" (side to side). What a life-filled action! However, as potent as the original idea was, this too can easily become a lifeless tradition. People can simply go through the motion with no heart or spirit. This can become a ritual with no meaning unless the inner self is engaged in the process.

My pastor is a phenomenal teacher. I have learned more from his teaching than from any other human being. A while ago on Sunday morning he made this statement: "A sinister blindness comes upon us as we get used to what goes on around us. Historically this has been considered one of the seven deadly sins, and it's labeled 'satiety.' When we have satiety, the best things in the world will not please us."[1] He's absolutely right! We "get used to what goes on around us," and we block it out. It loses its appeal. It becomes ho-hum. Old hat. Boring. Even the best things this world has to offer can become monotonous if we are immersed in them long enough.

The scientific term for this is the reticular activating system. It is what filters things out and causes us to not notice certain things to which we have become accustomed. It is the reason that our fifteen-year-old son can walk into his bedroom and not notice the mess that drives his mother absolutely crazy.

Before my wife and I were married and moved to another area, one of our favorite places to go on dates was a quaint Italian restaurant. Oddly, the restaurant was situated right next to some railroad tracks. I recall numerous times eating at the restaurant as a train went past. Everything in the dining room rattled as the locomotive and freight cars rumbled by. One incident in particular is still etched into my mind. Our server was standing at our table taking our order when the train rolled past. As usual, everything shook. We could feel it in our chairs. The water in our glasses splashed about. I was relatively sure that pictures were about to fall off the wall. I looked at the waitress and asked, "Do you ever get used to that?" She looked back at me and in all candidness replied, "Used to what?" She had become so accustomed to the vibrations that she had reached a point where she didn't even notice. Her reticular activating system had kicked in, and the train and its side effects were blocked out.

The same thing can happen to us in worship. We get together every week because...well, because it's what we do. We sing some songs, say some words, listen to the preacher, and then go home. Too often we've lost touch with the depth and meaning because we have become accustomed to the various aspects of the service. We go through the motions and miss the spirit of what we're doing.

Honest, biblical worship must engage more than our mouths and hands. It must come from the inner us, the heart, the spirit. Puritan Stephen Charnock lived during the seventeenth century, and he said it this way: "Without the heart, it is not worship; it is a stage play, an acting part.... We may be truly said to worship God, though we [lack] perfection; but we cannot be said to worship Him if we [lack] sincerity."[2] Charnock wrote this almost four hundred years ago, but he certainly hit the nail on the head for us today. It's not a matter of going through a prescribed ritual. Saying the right words and performing the correct physical actions are worthwhile only if the inner self is involved at the same time. Otherwise our worship is merely a stage play, an acting part.

Not long ago someone suggested that we should have a "reality meter" in our worship services. How would you like to be connected to a device that would register, preferably for all to see, whether or not you are actually worshiping or just going through the motions? Of course, it's not really possible. But if it actually were feasible to do such a thing, would you volunteer to have it hooked up to you? I didn't think so. Neither would I.

If we intend to worship in spirit, the question then is this: Do we really mean the words we say and sing? Are we just going through the motions, or are we honestly engaging the inner self—the spirit, the heart? Truly biblical worship is not simply an outward show. It must originate from within.

Worshiping in Truth

Although the origin of our worship clearly must come from the inside, we cannot fool ourselves into rationalizing that simply thinking some nice thoughts toward God is enough. Why not? Because Jesus also tells us that besides being about spirit, worship is about truth.

If we are going to worship in truth, we need to know what truth is. In John 17:17, Jesus said to His Father, "Your word is truth." The Bible is the revelation of God's truth to us about Him and His interaction with us. Therefore, if we are going to endeavor to worship in truth, we must use Scripture to define the boundaries for what is acceptable.

Many people in the Church today take more of their cues about what is acceptable in worship from their experiences in church as children instead of from what the Bible says. I am not suggesting that all of those experiences in church are necessarily wrong. However, they may not all be biblical.

Not long ago, at one of our worship seminars, someone gave me a note that said, "We cannot fully understand worship today unless we look at it from a historical perspective. The Christian Church has nearly 2,000 years of experience in worshiping God. We cannot disconnect our worship today from the worship of God that has gone on through the centuries."

Although I agree with the general gist of the statement, other factors must be considered. First, the fact that something has happened in the past—maybe even repeatedly—does not automatically make that thing biblical. Second, although being biblical and being historical are not necessarily exclusive of one another, Scripture is not just about history. It is also about today, here and now. The Bible is not a static book. The writer of Hebrews tells us, "For the word of God is living and active" (Hebrews 4:12). If we demand that Scripture speak only from the viewpoint of ancient history, we have relegated it to the same level as a history book. Rather, we must recognize that the Word of God speaks to us today, not just because of what has happened in the past but because it is relevant to us in our culture and society.

In light of this, our worship must be based on a biblical foundation, not a historical one. Yes, we should consider the historical record of Christian worship, but the bedrock foundation must be grounded solidly on God's Word. Otherwise, Jesus might just as well have been speaking to us when He quoted the prophet Isaiah, "In vain do they worship me, teaching as doctrines the commandments of men" (Matthew 15:9; Mark 7:7).

The true measuring rod for our worship must be the Word of God. Not our traditions. Not our culture. Not our experiences. If any of these usurp the position that Scripture alone should have, we have erred egregiously.

A few years ago I was ministering in a Christian (independent) church in a rather conservative area of the Midwest. The pastor of this church had previously pastored a church in a medium-sized city in Puerto Rico. His was the only English-speaking church in the city. Consequently English-speaking Christians of practically every background were in his church. Because of the diversity of backgrounds, church members had a variety of ideas about worship. For the sake of unity, this pastor wanted to get them all on the same page about worship, so he began months of personal study from the Word of God. He endeavored to go beyond his own background and culture, or even beyond what the culture in Puerto Rico might dictate, and look honestly at what the Bible has to say about worship. Once he had completed this monumental study, he began teaching the congregation what he had learned.

Sometime later he left that church in Puerto Rico and became the pastor of the Christian church where I encountered him. He informed me that shortly after coming to this church he had begun teaching the congregation the same things about worship. He told me that it took only two sermons before people started coming to him and asking questions like, "You're not turning this into a charismatic church are you?" As he told me this, he said, "I never even suggested such a possibility!"

Too often, though, people in our society have equated certain forms and expressions of worship with certain types of churches. If someone raises his or her hands or expresses an exuberant joy, many people have the idea that that person must be Pentecostal. Unfortunately, we have too often failed to recognize that many of those forms and expressions are not charismatic or Pentecostal or some other tradition. They are biblical. We have relied too much on our cultural bias and our traditions instead of looking honestly at what the Bible has to say about worship.

You may be aware that many third-world countries are experiencing a huge influx of people into the kingdom of God. Because so many people have come into a saving relationship with the Lord in such a short time, often the churches do not have the necessary leadership to disciple the new converts. As a result, a person who has been a Christian only a very short time sometimes becomes a pastor simply because no one else is available to fill that role. An organization that I know, International Leadership Training Institute, has developed basic biblical leadership curricula for third-world countries to assist those novice leaders.

Several years ago, as the institute was developing some of the early training materials, they asked me to help write the section on worship. I agreed but quickly realized that it was one of the most difficult undertakings I had ever attempted. Every word I wrote caused me to consider, "Is this biblical enough that it will help native Africans?" With each sentence I wondered, "Will this offer true scriptural benefit to some new leader in the tribal regions of Argentina?" It was during this process that I realized how much the American church has been affected by our culture. So much of what is taught in churches in our society has a cultural bias rather than a biblical one.

Throughout the ages, and in our society today, people have taken secular, cultural ideas and sprinkled them with scriptures. Oftentimes these ideas then become traditions. That's backward. The foundation—the beginning point—must be the Bible.

In Matthew 15 Jesus clearly explained the importance of God's Word over tradition:

> Then Pharisees and scribes came to Jesus from Jerusalem and said, "Why do your disciples break the tradition of the elders? For they do not wash their hands when they eat."
>
> He answered them, "And why do you break the commandment of God for the sake of your tradition? For God commanded, 'Honor your father and your mother,' and, 'Whoever reviles father or mother must

surely die.' But you say, 'If anyone tells his father or his mother, What you would have gained from me is given to God, he need not honor his father.' So for the sake of your tradition you have made void the word of God. You hypocrites! Well did Isaiah prophesy of you, when he said: 'This people honors me with their lips, but their heart is far from me; in vain do they worship me, teaching as doctrines the commandments of men.'" (Matthew 15:1–9)

Unfortunately, even today many churches substitute their own traditions—"This is the way we've always done it"—for the clear mandates of the Word of God. This is an all-too-common occurrence in our culture.

Please recognize that I'm not picking on any one particular tradition. I regularly minister in Bible-believing churches of nearly every background. Presbyterian and Pentecostal, Mennonite and Methodist, Baptist, Vineyard, Lutheran, Evangelical Free, and many more have all invited me to speak in their churches. My experience has shown that many Pentecostal churches may clap their hands and shout, but the people rarely kneel. However, lots of more conservative churches have kneeling down to a fine art, but the people rarely lift their hands.

It should be understood that all of these expressions are simply physical demonstrations of spiritual truths. Bowing our knees is a physical demonstration of bowing our hearts. Lifting our hands is a physical demonstration of lifting our hearts.

When I've explained some of these principles in churches, occasionally someone has said, "Hold on a minute. I don't do that emotionalism stuff!" My usual response is, "That's good!" You see, emotional*ism*—

where people live for and out of their emotional experiences—is wrong. Real emotions, however, are not a bad thing from God's perspective.

Many people in our culture struggle with this idea, especially those of us with a northern European background. Our white, North American culture has very little room for emotions. We're generally not given to expressing emotions very freely.

Have you noticed, though, that the people through whom God chose to reveal Himself, the Israelites, were not from northern Europe? They were from the Middle East, where expressing emotions is much more commonplace. If you want to see emotions expressed fully, go to a Jewish wedding! The people generally don't hold anything back. And these are the folks through whom we received the revelation about the Lord. That was not an accident on God's part.

Hear me clearly on this. I'm not talking about emotional*ism* but about true, heartfelt worship that includes all of our being. Jesus said, "And you shall love the Lord your God with *all* your heart and with *all* your soul and with *all* your mind and with *all* your strength" (Mark 12:30). That's not passive! Indeed, worship cannot be passive.

In his book *One Thing Needful*, Dr. Gary Mathena suggests that if the greatest commandment is to love God with all our heart, soul, and mind (Matthew 22:37–38), it follows that the greatest sin is to *not* love God with all our heart, soul, and mind. That is definitely a thought worth pondering.

What does it mean to love God with all our heart, mind, strength, and soul? I'm not certain I could accurately elaborate every nuance of Jesus' exact meaning in these words. This statement could be somewhat shaded and colored in many ways. I could, I think, read quite a lot into this declaration and still be within the scope of what Jesus was endeavoring to convey. However, no one could honestly read those words and think that a passive attitude could possibly be deemed acceptable. In light of Jesus' words, the very idea that a halfhearted, namby-pamby effort might be pleasing to God is ludicrous.

How would you respond if I told you that my wife and I have been married for more than twenty-five years but we really never *demonstrate* our feelings toward each other? We never offer a gentle, caring word or a compassionate touch or physical passion. We just live together. We believe in love. Certainly we believe we love each other. We just never demonstrate that love. (By the way, none of these things are true about the relationship between my wife and me.) If this is truly how we related, what would you say? I'm guessing you'd probably tell me that my marriage was in trouble.

In the same way, there is more to worshiping God than just thinking some nice thoughts toward Him. If this is all we ever do, we are missing much of the relationship He has described in His Word. Our relationship with Him, if we examine it honestly, may be in trouble.

Spirit *and* Truth

As you can see, true worship involves worshiping in spirit and worshiping in truth. Spirit—coming from the real us. Truth—following the mandates of God's Word. Both halves of that equation are essential.

If we have only spirit, our worship becomes completely experiential. We may show lots of emotion but have little (if any) biblical foundation. Our worship may well have plenty of excitement, passion, and sincerity, but the true scriptural basis is missing.

On the other hand, if we have just truth, we go through a ritual but without honesty. We may say proper words and go through biblically accurate motions yet neglect the heart. With truth only, we may have an appearance of theological correctness, but we miss the spirit of that theology. We can go through the motions out of a sense of duty and obligation: "This is what is expected of us."[3]

My wife loves fresh-cut flowers. Suppose, returning from a trip one day, I walk in the door of our home and hand her a bouquet of flowers. She might say, "Oh, honey, flowers. How sweet. Why did you bring me these?" If I responded, "Duty! I felt obligated to bring you those flowers," wouldn't that automatically diminish the gift?

Let's rewind and try that scene again. Suppose, returning from a trip one day, I walk in the door of our home and hand my wife a bouquet of flowers. She might say, "Oh, honey, flowers. How sweet. Why did you bring me these?" If this time I responded, "Because they are an expression of my love for you," wouldn't that change the entire scenario? Of course it would!

All of the actions must be merely physical demonstrations of spiritual truths. You and I both know that someone could kneel but still be standing on the inside. You may raise your hands but inside your fists may be clenched. The actions are important but only when motivated by a heart that is turned toward God. The Lord wants us to be biblically accurate in our worship (truth), but our worship must come from a heart that is turned toward Him (spirit).

chapter three

SPIRITUAL BLESSINGS AND PHYSICAL OBEDIENCE

*I*n the Old Testament, when Elisha the prophet was on his deathbed, Joash, king of Israel, went to visit him. Elisha told the king to shoot an arrow out the window, and the king did so. Afterward the prophet declared, "The LORD's arrow of victory, the arrow of victory over Syria!" (2 Kings 13:17). Though he was near death, Elisha was encouraging the king.

> And [Elisha] said, "Take the arrows," and [the king] took them. And he said to the king of Israel, "Strike the ground with them." And he struck three times and stopped. Then the man of God was angry with him and said, "You should have struck five or six times; then you would have struck down Syria until you had made an end of it, but now you will strike down Syria only three times." (2 Kings 13:18–19)

Why was Elisha so angry? Moments before he was enthusiastic. Why would the prophet become so obviously irritated with the king? There can be only one answer to that question. If Elisha did not specifically tell Joash what to do, there is just one reason for Elisha to be upset. What he expected Joash to do was obvious. Oh, maybe not to you and me. We live at a different time, in a different place, and we would not necessarily have the spiritual astuteness that would have been expected of the king of Israel.

The prophet was angry because the king had missed the obvious. Elisha's anger flared because Joash had failed to recognize that his physical actions had spiritual significance. Joash should have known that. Apparently he had a lapse of memory, and Elisha verbally assaulted the king.

Do you remember when Joshua and the Israelites were preparing to lay siege to Jericho? Do you remember what the Lord told them to do? He told them to march, blow trumpets, and shout, and the walls of the city would fall down. Right? And it happened just as God had promised (Joshua 6).

Let me ask a difficult, deeply theological, thought-provoking question. Do you suppose that there was any chance at all that the almighty, sovereign God of the universe could have caused the walls to fall flat without the people of Israel doing those things? Okay, maybe the question isn't actually very hard. Of course He could have! There can be no question that the Lord could have knocked the walls down without the Hebrews so much as moving or even breathing.

But He didn't.

God waited for the people to do what He told them to do before He did His part. Again, their physical actions had spiritual significance. When the Lord's people are obedient to do the things He tells them to do, they receive spiritual blessings from on high.

Perhaps you recall when the Israelites fought the Amalekites (Exodus 17:8–13). Moses stood on a hill overlooking the action. "Whenever Moses held up his hand, Israel prevailed, and whenever he lowered his hand, Amalek prevailed" (Exodus 17:11). When Moses got tired of holding up his arms, he sat down, and others held his hands up for him. Once again, there clearly was a spiritual significance to physical actions.

You might wonder why God chose to do this. Why did the Lord decide to attach such spiritual significance to these physical actions? I'll be honest. I really don't know. I'm not God. If I *were* God, I might not have chosen to do this. However, He didn't ask for my opinion. Or yours. What I do know is that Scripture contains simply too much evidence to deny the fact that the Lord offers spiritual blessings to those who are physically obedient to His Word.

In his letter to the saints at Rome, Paul said, "I appeal to you therefore, brothers, by the mercies of God, to present your bodies as a living sacrifice, holy and acceptable to God, which is your spiritual worship" (Romans 12:1). Present your body. Give yourself to God. Offer yourself as a living sacrifice to the Lord. Doing this "is your spiritual worship." The physical turns to spiritual. It happens again and again throughout the pages of Scripture.

We must recognize that the spiritual is more real—more eternally significant—than the natural, or sensory, realm. God is more interested in our hearts than our physical actions. However, when we follow the physical actions that have been mandated by God, spiritual blessings are associated with them.

Whether you or I like it or not—whether you or I understand it or not—makes no difference. God gives spiritual blessings when we involve ourselves in the physical actions commanded in His Word. This includes our worship of Him. When we follow the physical actions that have been mandated by the Lord, spiritual significance is associated with them. If this is true in life in general, it is certainly true in worship.

How Should We Worship?

I mentioned earlier that most people in our society, even in the Church, don't really understand worship. Too many ideas about worship are based on our experiences or our traditions. Consequently, people need to learn *how* to worship. In her book *Up with Worship*, Anne Ortlund said it this way: "Worshipers all have to be taught how to worship.... Let none of us assume we know how. In fact, scenes of heaven in the book of Revelation seem so foreign to us we probably know much less than we think we know."[1]

Although my father was a kind man, I have almost no recollections of his demonstrating affection toward me. I do not remember him hugging me past the age of six or seven, and I cannot recall him ever telling me he loved me. This is a very different scenario from my current relationship with my teenage boys. We regularly hug, and we frequently tell each other, "I love you." Because of my upbringing, though, this was not natural for me. These things are right and important for a father's relationship with his children, but they were not an innate part of me. I had to learn to do them. Similarly, we need to learn how to worship. It is not usually something we get by osmosis.

In fact, for most of us, much of what we think we know probably needs to be unlearned.

As I mentioned earlier, my wife and I have been married for more than twenty-five years. Because we have been together for so long, I think I have a pretty good idea about what she likes and dislikes. What would happen, though, if one day I discovered a list she had written but had never given to me. This list contained things I could do to really please her. Perhaps she included suggestions about ways to communicate better or things she likes that I had never considered. If such a list existed, what would happen if I simply ignored it? After all, I've been at this for a long time. I don't need her suggestions. I already know what works. Why would I want that silly list?

My hope is that this scenario—my refusal to pay any heed to such a list—sounds far-fetched to you. However, if this actually happened, it is not just my wife who would be less fulfilled in the relationship. I would also be adversely affected. If she makes it clear exactly what she wants and I refuse to pay any heed to her desires, doesn't that say something about my love—or lack of love—for her?

In the same way, God has given us some very specific directives in His Word about *how* we should worship Him. The Lord has made it very clear that He has preferences about the manner in which we worship. Sadly, there are people who have been in church practically their entire lives who look at some of those directives and respond, "But we've never done it that way before." These people are convinced that their way is the "correct" way, even though God's Word offers evidence to the contrary. Such people will be impoverished in their relationship with God because they have ignored what He wants.

Expressing ourselves through physical actions—sometimes wordless physical actions—is a common occurrence even in our society today. Walk up to someone you meet for the first time (or even someone you've known for many years) and extend your hand. That person will almost unquestionably shake hands with you. It requires no prompting. You don't need to say, "Let's shake hands." We just do this because it is a common way we express greetings in our culture. Shaking hands is a wordless physical action that has significance in our society.

Many other wordless physical actions have meaning for us. A kiss. A salute. A wave of the hand. All of these, and many other physical actions, have significance for us in our culture. The people of every civilization have various types of physical ways they express themselves. Understanding this, the question we should consider is, What are the physical ways we should interact with God in His kingdom? In other words, what does the Bible say about *how* we should worship? A thorough study through the entire Bible would take far more time and space than this small book would allow, so we'll look at just some of the expressions listed in the Bible's hymnbook, Psalms.

Psalm 46:10: "Be still, and know that I am God." The wristwatch I wear is battery-powered, but it ticks like a windup watch. I can never actually hear it ticking, though, except at night. During the day, even though it is never more than a few feet (and sometimes just a few inches) from my ear, it produces no noticeable sound. If you asked me during the day amidst the hubbub of daily life or even the seemingly quiet hum of my computer, I would swear to you that my watch makes no noise at all. At night, however, when all of the competing sounds are absent, the ticking is thunderous, sometimes keeping me awake. Similarly, we occasionally need to rid ourselves of the uproarious tumult of everyday life and learn to *be still,* listening intently to the Lord. This is a foreign idea in our society. Too often we have a hurry-up mentality. Go here. Go there. Do this. Do that.

Be still?! What's that? We would do well to learn to *be still* and know that He is God.

Psalm 47:1: "Clap your hands, all peoples!" I was at a conference where the person in charge quoted this verse and said that this Hebrew word for clap is talking about applause, not clapping along with the music. Sometime later I was at another conference where the person in charge quoted this verse and said that this Hebrew word for clap is talking about clapping along with the music, not applause. Hmmm. Those guys could not have both been correct!

The truth is that the Hebrew word used for clap in this verse is not that specific. The word could have either meaning. If you want to honor God by clapping along with the music, go ahead. At the same time, the Lord is far more worthy than any human being you will ever applaud. Go ahead and clap for Him.

Clap your hands.

Psalm 66:1: "Shout for joy to God." I have encountered churches that would never consider this possibility. Why not?

"We don't do that in this church."

"But it's in the Bible."

"Well, yes, but we just don't do that here."

"But it's scriptural."

"Sorry, not here."

Please understand that I am not suggesting that you should shout to God in every service. The Bible does not say that. However, to be completely unwilling ever to "shout for joy to God" goes beyond Scripture. We take too many of our cues of what is acceptable from what our traditions have taught us instead of what the Bible says.

Shout for joy to God.

Psalm 95:6: "Oh come, let us worship and bow down; let us kneel before the LORD, *our Maker!"* It seems to me that there are few things our fleshly nature dislikes more than being humbled. By nature we are proud, haughty, even arrogant. We want our way. The idea of humbling ourselves is outside our scope of normal thinking. But that's exactly why we need to do it.

When we kneel or bow before the Lord, we are physically acknowledging that there is One who is greater than we are. The apostle Paul says, "I bow my knees before the Father" (Ephesians 3:14).

Is it essential for us to kneel or bow down in every service? No. Again, the Bible does not say that. Yet kneeling is indeed a powerfully humbling way to demonstrate that we are but the creature. God is the all-powerful Creator. We humble ourselves and acknowledge the greatness of the Lord by bowing down and kneeling.

Bow down and kneel before the Lord, our Maker!

Psalm 96:1: "Oh sing to the LORD *a new song."* Have you ever noticed that the Bible never once tells us to sing an *old* song? Come on, smile. I was merely making a joke. But it's true.

If you have read other books that I've written, you know that I talk a lot about the importance of using old hymns. Many churches have thrown them out, much to their own detriment. There is a depth to some of those old songs that we need in the church today. However, we also need new songs.

It is not as though God ever gets tired of our words of praise to Him. We, on the other hand, get tired of saying or singing those words in exactly the same way over and over. We need a newness, a freshness in our worship.

Sing a new song to the Lord.

Psalm 134:2: "Lift up your hands to the holy place and bless the LORD!" (see also Psalm 63:4). Many years ago a wonderful movie entitled *Sergeant York* was made. It is a remarkable, true story about a guy from the hills of Tennessee who was a sergeant during World War I. The young man went to Europe to fight and single-handedly captured an entire German platoon.

At one point during the movie, the captured Germans marched along with their hands in the air. What does that mean? Surrender.

Do you ever sense a need to do that with God? Try raising your hands to God and saying, "Lord, I surrender. I belong to You. I'm not my own. I was bought with a price [1 Corinthians 7:23]. I surrender to You anew and afresh here and now. I'm Yours."

Lift up your hands.

Psalm 149:3: "Let them praise his name with dancing" (see also Psalm 150:4; 2 Samuel 6:14). Some have suggested that this Hebrew word for dancing specifically refers to a choreographed, planned dance. This would be akin to what today is commonly called liturgical dance—trained dancers doing their best to honor the Lord with skills and abilities. Others have said that this Hebrew word refers to a spontaneous, kick-up-your-heels kind of dance. A joyful jig. A holy hop. A jubilant expression of joy to God.

Here, again, the Hebrew word is not so specific. It can have either meaning.

If we ask the instrumentalists in church to work at their art form (music), there is clearly a place to ask those who have been trained in the art of dance to work at their craft for the glory of God. At the same time, there are moments when we just need to kick up our heels in a grand expression of celebration and honor God with all we are.

Praise God with *dancing*.

Psalm 150:3–5: "Praise him with trumpet sound...with lute and harp...with tambourine...with strings and pipe...with sounding cymbals." Some have suggested that since the Bible does not specifically mention certain instruments (e.g., drums, electric guitars, electronic keyboards, saxophones), those instruments are not acceptable for worship. Okay everyone, break out those lutes and harps!

Seriously, these verses, as well as other sections of the Bible, speak of specific instruments that were available in that time and place. This does not mean that such lists are exclusive of instruments available to us today. Please note, though, that various types of instruments are listed. Stringed instruments, wind instruments, and percussion instruments are all mentioned.

If this list was truly exclusive, pay close attention to what is not listed. There is no mention of pianos or pipe organs. Actually, neither of these is mentioned anywhere in the pages of Scripture.[2]

Here's the truth. If these verses had been written today, they would most likely include such things as drums, electric guitars, electronic keyboards, and saxophones as well as pipe organs and pianos.

Praise God with a *variety of musical instruments*.

All of these passages and explanations help us more fully understand the *truth* side of worship. What does the Word of God—not our culture or traditions or (and this is very important) even our own preferences—say about *how* we are to express our worship to the Lord? True worshipers will worship God in spirit and according to the truth of His Word. Scripture seems clear that worship often involves various forms of action in our physical bodies.

chapter four

OUR WORSHIP IS FOR GOD

Our church has a dedicated team of people who handle the technology aspects (sound, video projection, etc.) of our services. Some time ago, because of a special presentation, one of the members of this team was at church very early on Sunday morning. My guess is that he left home that day even before his kids were out of bed. When the rest of the family arrived at the church, the service had just begun. I'll never forget seeing five-year-old Hope walking down the main aisle and looking back and forth. She scanned the congregation, looking very intently for something or someone. Because the people were all standing, she didn't see right away what she was looking for. Suddenly, she got to a point where she had a perfect sight line to her father. Her face lit up, her arms went up, and she ran to Daddy.

I found it interesting that it didn't seem to bother Hope that others watched her do that. She apparently didn't care in the least that others were observing her actions. What she did was not for those other people. It was for Daddy.

That's the point. Our worship is for God. It is not a show for others. It is an activity in which we are involved that both honors God and is directed toward God. There can be only one object of our worship: the Lord Most High. He is the only One to whom our worship is directed.

Let's look at the same idea from a different angle. Until the time of Jesus, the Ark of the Covenant was the single most significant object on the face of the earth. The Ark was where God chose to make Himself known to mankind. It was in and through the Ark that the Lord revealed Himself to the inhabitants of Earth. This was the place where God had promised to meet with His people and speak to them (Exodus 25:22). In Old Testament times, the Ark was essentially the representation of the Lord's presence on earth.

At one point, the Israelites' most persistent enemy—the Philistines—captured the Ark of God. They decided that it was quite a trophy, and they put it into their pagan temple with their god Dagon. Dagon fell over! I love it! He just toppled right over, smack down onto the floor. So they stood him back up. He fell over again, and this time his head came off! Even this stone "god" knew to whom he should bow.

These folks had no idea what they'd latched on to. They thought that the Ark was just a nifty little trinket from the Israelite temple. What they actually got was the place where God's Spirit resided.

The Ark was actually in the land of the Philistines for seven months. The representation of God's presence was gone from the land of Israel for more than half a year. Try to imagine the scene when the Ark of God was returned to Israel. The Lord was no longer going to be absent from His people. The Ark was being restored to its rightful place. Excitement filled the air. A celebration was the appropriate response. And a procession, a parade, seemed like a fitting and proper way to welcome the Ark back home.

That's just what the people did. They had a parade. Do you recall who led the parade? It was David, the king of Israel. Further, do you happen to remember what he was doing as he led the parade? He walked along stoically, saying, in a monotone voice, something like, "I thank You, Lord, that Your presence is being returned to Your people." Right? No way! David danced and celebrated. He was genuinely excited to welcome the return of the Lord's presence. The representation of God's dwelling place was coming back to His people, and David publicly demonstrated his enthusiasm.

At the same time, though, do you recall the reaction of David's wife to his dancing? She wasn't too happy with his actions. (Read the story for yourself in 2 Samuel 6:16–22.) For Michal, such a display was definitely over the top. David apparently was not dissuaded by her comments, though. He said, "I will make merry before the LORD. I will make myself yet more contemptible than this, and I will be abased in your eyes" (2 Samuel 6:21–22). May I distill his words to their essence? "Honey, it wasn't for you. It was for God."

Our worship isn't for the other humans who might want to watch us. It is for the Lord. Those who would rather watch than worship are already on the outside looking in. Focus on God, not on people.

Many years ago when I was working with *Psalmist* magazine, one of my many jobs was that of photographer.

One day I was shooting candid photos during a special evening worship service. I remember well a young woman worshiping with outstretched arms, closed eyes, and a countenance that bespoke the love she had for her Savior. I was several feet in front of her with my camera pointed directly at her when she suddenly opened her eyes. Immediately realizing what I was doing, she quickly closed her eyes, lifted her hands even higher, and broke into an ear-to-ear smile. The shot I had wanted was now completely lost. Instead of worshiping, the woman was now posing for the camera.

Are there ever times during worship when you are more concerned with your persona than with focusing your affections on God? It is all too easy to get caught up in what those around us think instead of simply worshiping the Lord. My worship—your worship—is not for those around us. It is for God.

Pharisees and Spider Webs

Perhaps you recall when Jesus went to the home of Simon the Pharisee for supper. While Jesus was seated at the table, an unnamed sinful woman came in and washed His feet with her tears and hair, kissed His feet, and anointed them with a very expensive perfume. Simon thought it was dreadful that Jesus would allow such a person to touch Him, so Jesus did what Jesus often did. He told a story.

> "A certain moneylender had two debtors. One owed five hundred denarii, and the other fifty. When they could not pay, he canceled the debt of both. Now which of them will love him more?" Simon answered,

"The one, I suppose, for whom he canceled the larger debt." And he said to him, "You have judged rightly." (Luke 7:41–43)

Simon the Pharisee understood the point of Jesus' story from a cerebral perspective, but he completely missed the heart. Simon was not about to offer such an extravagant act of worship, because he had never allowed the grace and mercy of the Lord to touch him in the places he needed it most. He was not going to do what that woman did, because he had not experienced what she had experienced.

I live out in the country. Actually, as one person who visited my home told me, I don't live in the country—I live *past* country. In such a beautiful rural setting, I love to go for walks. The scenery is wonderful, and communing with the One who created such beauty is even better.

One gorgeous summer day I was out walking. The sun must have been at the wrong angle, because before I knew what was happening, I had walked under the overhanging branch of a large oak tree right into a huge spider web! Yuck! It was awful. I flailed around there on the road, trying to get all that sticky stuff off me. My legs and arms gyrated wildly. I ran my hands through my hair. I wiped my face and arms. Over and over again I retraced the same places, making absolutely certain that none of that disgusting web remained anywhere on me. Come on, be honest. In the same situation, you would have done the same thing. Right?

When I finally felt as though I had pretty well removed all of the foreign substance, I began walking again. It was then that I noticed a man standing on a hill a little way off. And much to my chagrin, he was staring right at me. Talk about life's most embarrassing moments!

It occurred to me that if *I* did not see the spider web and had walked right into it, certainly he could not have seen the spider web from where he was standing. All he saw from his vantage point was a guy on the road flailing around like a maniac. I must have been quite a sight! He could not have understood what I was doing, because he had not experienced what I had experienced. It was the same as the scenario with Simon the Pharisee and the sinful woman. Simon could not understand the woman's actions, because he had not experienced what she had experienced.

In light of this, we must be very careful to not allow our traditions—"I've never done it that way before"—to cause us to sit in judgment against our brothers or sisters in Christ. We cannot see their heart. As long as their form of worship has an honest, biblical basis, we must allow them the freedom to worship God as they choose. As I have mentioned previously, worship must be directed toward God. It is not for the watchers. It is for the King.

I recently attended a conference at which one speaker said he had become weary of hearing the word *worship* used as though it were an entity in and of itself. He told us there should be a law that the word *worship* must always be used in conjunction with the word *God* or *Lord* or some such reference to the Deity. Whereas I think this may be an overstatement, the man does have a point. Our worship must be directed to the One who ultimately is worthy of all worship: God. Anything less is not really worship.

chapter five

WORSHIP AS PART OF LIFE

*J*esus said, "But the hour is coming, and is now here, when the true worshipers will worship the Father in spirit and truth, for the Father is seeking such people to worship him" (John 4:23).

For many years I thought this passage said that the Father was looking for worship. Then one day when I read it again, I realized that this is not what Jesus was saying. He didn't use the word for the action. He used the word for the person. God is seeking *worshipers*. He is not so much interested in our coming in on Sunday morning and singing some pretty songs and saying some nice words. He's looking for a people whose lives reflect worship in all they say and all they do.

To truly become one of those worshipers the Lord is seeking, we must recognize that worship is not just a Sunday-morning activity. Of course you may be thinking,

"That's right, we do it Sunday night and Wednesday night too." If so, you're missing the point.

The apostle Paul wrote, "Present your bodies as a living sacrifice, holy and acceptable to God, which is your spiritual worship" (Romans 12:1). I like to think of doing this on a daily basis. What would happen if each day when you got out of bed, you were to declare, "Lord, today I'm Yours. Whatever I do, wherever I go, I want my life to bring honor and glory to You"? What do you suppose might be the end result if every person in your congregation did that for six days and then gathered together on the seventh day? Do you think there might be a bit of a difference in your corporate worship? Of course there would!

There is a quandary, though. Someone once said, "The problem with a living sacrifice is that it keeps crawling off the altar." This is true. We seem to have a natural tendency away from offering ourselves to God rather than toward it. Because of this, we need to be all the more vigilant in daily offering ourselves to the Lord. It's not a once-and-for-all offering. We must remind ourselves to keep it up. Otherwise we crawl off the altar and are gone just that quickly. Keep presenting yourself to the Lord so that it becomes a good habit. Give yourself to Him regularly to be that living sacrifice.

Doing All to the Glory of God

Scripture tells us, "Whatever you do, do all to the glory of God" (1 Corinthians 10:31). *Whatever you do.* That's pretty all-inclusive. *Do all to the glory of God.* When I was in school, "all" meant...all. Do all to the glory of God.

Whether you're at home, or on your job, or in the marketplace, or at school, doing all that you do to God's glory ultimately is worship unto Him.

A medieval monk named Brother Lawrence coined the phrase "practicing the presence of God." In his writings, Brother Lawrence states that when it was time for prayer in the monastery where he lived, such prayer time would often interrupt his worship of God in washing the dishes. He did *all* to the glory of God.

Someone emailed me the following story several years ago. I am unsure of the origin, but it is quite appropriate for this topic.

A professor was flying home after an exhausting weekend. He was tired and just wanted to be left alone. However, the flight attendant was so polite and helpful he finally said to her, "Delta Airlines is fortunate to have you working for them."

Her response stunned him. "Sir, my real employer is not Delta Airlines. I work for Jesus Christ. He is the greatest of all bosses."

Hmm. That sounds like doing all to the glory of God.

An accurate understanding of worship as part of everyday life fits the biblical definition of worship we discussed earlier—that worship honors God, is directed toward God, and requires involvement on our part. If we're doing all that we do to the *glory of God*, what we do honors God. If we're doing it *to* the glory of God, what we do is directed toward God. If *we're doing it*, obviously we're involved.

Not long ago I heard about a man who decided to brush his teeth just once a week. I know that sounds really disgusting, but let me explain. He had heard that dentists recommend brushing three times a day for about three minutes each time. He reasoned that three times per day times three minutes each time would be nine minutes per day. Multiply that by seven days and he would be brushing sixty-three minutes each week. Therefore, he thought that if he brushed just once a week for about an hour, he would accomplish the same thing.

He made the decision that each Sunday morning he would brush his teeth for an hour. He tried it the very next Sunday and quickly realized that there were certain issues he had not considered. The plaque that builds up on the teeth is much more easily removed with regular, three-times-per-day brushing than by trying to remove an entire week's worth of buildup at once. Additionally, the man had not considered how sore his gums would be after a full hour of brushing. He had brushed for only twenty minutes when his raw and bleeding gums forced him to stop. Further, he also had not given much thought to what his breath would smell like if he hadn't brushed his teeth in several days. He noticed that people seemed to keep their distance from him. After just one attempt, he realized the idea was simply not going to work.

Sadly, many people attempt this same type of process in worship. They ignore God for six days and then go to church to "worship" on Sunday morning. The worldly mindset that has built up over an entire week of avoiding the Lord will not likely be eradicated in one hour on Sunday. Not exercising spiritual muscles on your own during the week will render them useless in the corporate setting.

In his book *Your God Is Too Safe*, Mark Buchanan said it like this: "If Sunday for one hour is the only time we worship, no wonder we do it sloppily, haltingly, hastily, and leave as hungry as we came. If we only ate one day a week, and on that day only one meal, we would die soon enough. And man does not live on bread alone. Robust worshipers worship in spirit and in truth. They don't need a temple. The kitchen will do."[1]

Worship Each Day

Nearly twenty-five years ago Ronald Allen and Gordon Borror wrote *Worship: Rediscovering the Missing Jewel.* In that classic, Allen and Borror state it this way: "The real factor in worship is a heart desire for God; the reason it fails to occur in the pew is [that] it fails to occur in the daily routine of living."[2]

Dr. Judson Cornwall once said, "If there's been no song in your heart for six days, there won't be one on the seventh." Like brushing your teeth just once a week, worshiping only once a week won't work.

Years ago I heard a man preaching about the importance of the Word of God. In his message he quoted several verses from Psalm 119. This made sense, since nearly every verse in Psalm 119 talks about the Word. One verse in particular that he quoted really made me think. "Seven times a day I praise you for your righteous rules" (Psalm 119:164). After he read the verse he mentioned the importance of praising God for His Word. Specifically, he mentioned the part about praising the Lord seven times a day. As I sat listening, I thought, *He's right. We should praise God seven times a day for His Word.* But then I wondered, *Lord, do we praise You seven times a day for anything? And if we did, would it make a difference in our lives?*

I have a rather vivid imagination (actually I've been told that I have an overactive imagination), so when I read something like this—"seven times a day"—it is quite normal for me to figure out how to make it a reality. How about this for an idea?

1. when we get up in the morning
2. at breakfast
3. midmorning
4. at lunchtime
5. midafternoon
6. at suppertime
7. before we go to bed

What would happen, do you suppose, if you and I took a few moments at each of those times every day and gave thanks and praise to God? I am not necessarily talking about for His Word. You can pick any topic you like. Giving thanks and praise is the important part.

I am not suggesting that it is essential to make a liturgy out of praising the Lord seven times a day. (Although, because we have a tendency to become complacent with the things of God, something so radical could wake us up a bit.) Instead it should be more of an attitude. We should be the most thankful, praising people on earth. Set aside the material blessings of the nation in which we live. The fact is that the death and resurrection of the Lord Jesus Christ means that you and I will spend eternity in heaven with God. That alone should be enough for us to give thanks and praise to Him every moment of every day for the rest of our lives.

Some time ago I was a guest speaker at a large church on a Sunday morning. During the sermon I happened to quote Psalm 119:164: "Seven times a day I praise you." After the service, the missions pastor from the church approached me. He said, "You know, Tom, that 'seven times a day' idea is very interesting. We look at the

Muslims and think they are really fanatical because five times a day they bow down toward Mecca and pray. Do you know why they do that?"

I assured him I had no idea.

"The reason they do that is that when Mohammed was starting the Muslim religion, it was the practice of the Christians to pray seven times a day. Mohammed said, 'That's too many. We will just do five.'"

I was stunned. That puts the whole concept in a different perspective. I think God is looking for some fanatics today, some people who will live the Christian life full on, all the way through, praising God wherever they are all through the day.

Another time when I had been a guest speaker at a church, I received a letter from a man in the congregation shortly after my visit. The man told me that after hearing me speak, he decided to set the alarm on his digital watch to beep every hour during the day. Each time the alarm went off, he was being reminded to praise the Lord. What a great idea! Make worship part of everyday life.

When worship *is* part of everyday life, it alters the way we view corporate worship. It is no longer a time when we expect the worship leader to pump us up after a draining week. Instead, it becomes our natural response.

Respected preacher and theologian G. Campbell Morgan (1863–1945) once commented that the worship of the sanctuary—our corporate gathering of worship— is meaningless unless it is preceded by six days of worship as a way of life. If we truly understand the grace of God, this statement is a bit strong. Nevertheless, it has a great deal of merit. We cannot go out and live our lives in any manner we wish for six days and then, at the end of six days, gather together for corporate worship. Ultimately a weekly corporate assembly of worship should be the culmination of a whole week of worship lived in everyday life. As a group, we should be taking the entire week of everyday worship and offering it all to the Lord. Living a life of worship clearly will affect our corporate worship of God.

Here's an interesting thought to ponder. A music teacher knows immediately how much a student has been diligent with the music during the week by what he or she hears in the first few minutes. I've sometimes wondered whether the same is true for God and our worship. Have we been diligent to "practice" during the week, or are we content to leave worship until we all gather corporately?

In his tape series *Worship: A Biblical View*, Charles Stanley says this: "If our purpose in life is to glorify God (keep in mind that we have seven days per week and 24 hours per day or 168 hours per week), isn't it ridiculous for us to think that God would be happy with one hour on Sunday morning?" Of course it is.

I once heard someone say that our actions betray who we really are. The things we do in everyday life depict the real us. It seems backward to me that we could have the attitude, "O Holy, Righteous, Ever-present, All-powerful, All-knowing, Eternal God...all the time I have for You is one hour on Sunday morning." Of course, we would never actually say this, but unfortunately, that is too often how we act.

To become true worshipers, we must make worship an active, vital part of daily life. Worship is not just a once-a-week activity. True worshipers engage with God in worship each day, throughout the day.

chapter six

GLIMPSING THE GREATNESS OF GOD

*I*f you honestly desire to become a true worshiper, it is essential that you recognize who God is. We may think we understand, but in reality we do not. Our perception of God is far too small.

The story goes that Thomas Aquinas, perhaps the world's greatest theologian, toward the end of his life suddenly stopped writing. When his secretary complained that his work was unfinished, Thomas replied: "Brother Reginald, when I was at prayer a few months ago, I experienced something of the reality of Jesus Christ. That day, I lost all appetite for writing. In fact, all I have ever written about Christ seems now to me to be like straw."[1]

Almost anything we think we understand about God most likely falls light-years short of reality.

Twenty-five years ago Robert Bailey wrote a book entitled *New Ways in Christian Worship*. In it he said this: "We cannot worship rightly until we recapture, as the principle element of worship, the overwhelming sense of awe and reverence in the presence of God."[2] I love that phrase: "recapture...the overwhelming sense of awe and reverence in the presence of God." We desperately need that in our churches—and in our lives—today. We need to once again grab hold of that reverence for and awe of God. Why? Because when we do, the natural outcome will be worship.

Here's a regrettable fact: In our society, once we've done something once or twice it becomes old hat to us. Our usual reaction today to practically anything in life is, "Been there, done that." We're always looking for a product that is "new and improved." Last year's model is not good enough for us. Too often, we're bored unless we have something brand-new with the latest bells and whistles.

What do you suppose would be the response of Wilbur and Orville Wright if they took a ride on a modern jet? Their first flight was the equivalent distance of the wingspan of a modern Boeing 747. What would it be like for them to actually fly on such a plane? We, on the other hand, get on that plane and open a book or magazine to keep from being bored, or we grab a pillow and take a nap. We do anything at all to keep from being bored, because we've been there and done that. It's old news to us.

Our corporate worship gatherings can end up the same way. We do the same things over and over, and those things become old news to us. We need to recapture that sense of awe and reverence in the presence of God. When we do, the natural response will be worship.

Psalm 92:4 says this: "For you, O LORD, have made me glad by your work; at the works of your hands I sing for joy." Although I don't normally switch back and forth between various translations while I'm teaching, I recently encountered the New Living Translation's rendering of this verse and found it thought provoking. "You thrill me, LORD, with all you have done for me! I sing for joy because of what you have done" (Psalm 92:4). What a great attitude. You *thrill* me, Lord! The psalmist seems to have a handle on reverence for and awe of God. He was thrilled by God, and in response, he worshiped.

The Way We React to God

Do you recall the encounter between Elijah and the prophets of Baal on Mt. Carmel? In front of the people of Israel, Elijah issued a challenge to the prophets of the false god Baal. "Let two bulls be given to us, and let them choose one bull for themselves and cut it in pieces and lay it on the wood, but put no fire to it. And I will prepare the other bull and lay it on the wood and put no fire to it. And you call upon the name of your god, and I will call upon the name of the LORD, and the God who answers by fire, he is God" (1 Kings 18:23–24). The people agreed.

They did everything exactly as Elijah had said. Baal's prophets prepared their sacrifice and called out to their god. From morning until evening they called on Baal, but nothing happened. Finally, it was Elijah's turn. As if to really prove the point, he had his helpers repeatedly pour large jars of water on his sacrifice. He then stepped up and prayed that the Lord would show the people that He was indeed God. And the Lord did. Fire came down from heaven. The bull, the wood, the stones, the soil, and even the water were all consumed by the fire.

To me the response of the people really says it all. "When all the people saw it, they fell on their faces and said, 'The LORD, he is God; the LORD, he is God.'" (1 Kings 18:39). No one needed to tell them what to do or how to respond. They fell on their faces and worshiped the one true God. Worship is the natural response when we encounter the Lord.

The Bible is filled with similar illustrations of man's reaction to God. For example, the gospels of Matthew, Mark, and John all relate the incident of Jesus walking on the water. By the time this happened, some of the disciples had already been with Jesus for quite a while. They had even seen Him perform numerous miracles. However, that night when they saw Jesus walking across the water, something surely must have happened in their hearts and minds. Keep in mind that some of these guys were fishermen. They knew well the properties of water. They were keenly aware that one does not walk on water. When they saw Jesus walking *on* the water, they suddenly realized that this was not just an especially gifted man—this was God. Their response? "And those in the boat worshiped him, saying, 'Truly you are the Son of God'" (Matthew 14:33). They didn't require anyone to tell them what to do. The awe of and reverence for God were recaptured, and their immediate response was to worship Him.

In the ninth chapter of the Gospel of John, the story is told of a man who was born blind. One day Jesus healed the man. Actually Jesus made some mud, put it on the man's eyes, and told the man to go and wash off the mud. When the man did, although he was an adult, for the first time in his entire life, he was able to see. Can you even begin to imagine that experience? When the man's sight was miraculously granted, Jesus actually was nowhere around. Later, though, He sought out the man. Jesus asked the man if he believed in Him. Here's how Scripture depicts the response: "He said, 'Lord, I believe,' and *he worshiped him*" (John 9:38). No one needed to tell this man what to do. He had witnessed the miracle-working power of God made manifest through Jesus—he definitely recaptured an awe of and reverence toward the Lord—and his only possible response was to worship Him.

In one of his hymns, John Newton stated it this way:

> Weak is the effort of my heart
>   and cold my warmest thought,
> but when I see Thee as Thou art
>   I'll praise Thee as I ought.

When we take our first steps into heaven, we will not need anyone to tell us what to do. No classes will be necessary. We will need no instruction manuals. When we gaze upon God in all His glory, our only possible response will be to worship Him. That will be true in a time that is coming, yet the same is true here and now, perhaps less in degree, but no less in truth. When we get a glimpse of the Lord's greatness and majesty, His power, and His holiness, the natural human response is, "I want to worship a God like that!" When we recapture the sense of awe and reverence in the presence of God, it will cause us to worship.

So, the important question at this point is, How do we "recapture…the overwhelming sense of awe and reverence in the presence of God"? The answer is, we "see" Him.

Acts 2:25 tells us, "David says concerning [God], 'I saw the Lord always before me, for he is at my right hand that I may not be shaken.'" What an interesting statement. "I *saw* the Lord." Did David literally *see* the Lord? Of course not. However, he chose to perceive God all around him. David filled the frame of his mind with the Lord so no room was left for other things. We, also, need to focus on God.

The problem is that most people in today's society have much too flat, too mundane a perception of what God is like. Some time ago a survey was conducted among people who had previously attended church or who had visited churches. The question was asked directly, "Why don't you go to church now?" The two most common answers were that they found it boring and they found it irrelevant. Here's the truth: If we truly encounter the God of the Bible, we will never find Him boring, and we will never find Him irrelevant. Like those on Mount Carmel with Elijah, we might fall on our faces. It is even conceivable that we might run away in terror. Possibly we might be transfixed, immobilized by God's resplendent beauty. However, we could not possibly find Him either boring or irrelevant.

A while back I read an article that suggested that we do people a great disservice by encouraging them to come to church in fancy clothes and pretty hats. The author thought that issuing crash helmets at the door and having seat belts on the pews might be a better idea. Why? Because if we truly encounter the God of Scripture, our nice outfits could get rumpled. If the mountains begin to quake and the hills start to melt (Nahum 1:5), we might be much more comfortable wearing crash helmets and seat belts.

Focusing on God

Several years ago our oldest son wanted a pair of binoculars. Desiring to be a good steward of the finances entrusted to our family, I went to a pawnshop to see if I could find a quality pair of binoculars at a good price. Oddly, this particular pawnshop had just one set of binoculars in stock. As I checked them over, I found they had apparently been damaged. No matter what I did—I attempted every possible adjustment—both sides would not focus at the same time.

In much the same way, since mankind's fall into sin, God seems out of focus to us. He appears a bit blurry. What we need, then, is something to bring Him into focus. The special focusing tool we require is the Bible. Scripture is where we get the clear picture of the Lord.

Interestingly, everyone apparently has some idea about what God is like. Some picture God as the tyrant, the ogre in the sky, waiting to pounce on them the moment they do anything wrong. Others see Him as a grandfatherly type, a larger-than-life Santa Claus handing out precious treasures to the deserving. Still others see the Lord as simply an overgrown person, an immense version of themselves. Seemingly everyone has some idea in his or her mind of what God is like.

Unfortunately, even the image of God that most *Christians* entertain in their minds is far from the truth of the Scriptures. Christian author and teacher Josh McDowell said it this way: "Many times we do not put into context when we praise and worship God, what is true about God. Rather we worship a figment of our imagination influenced by a cafeteria eclectic theology."[3] Josh is right. Most people, even followers of Christ, have a blurry picture of God. Why? Because they have taken bits and pieces from the Bible and added some other ideas. The movie they saw a couple of years ago adversely affected their view of God's sovereignty. A conversation with their Uncle Jim changed for the worse how they see the Lord's love. Any number of things can help produce that "cafeteria eclectic theology" that blurs one's picture of God. To alleviate this, we need to focus on the real picture found in His Word.

The God Who Named Every Star

To help clarify what I am endeavoring to convey, let me offer a couple of simple examples from Scripture. First, in Isaiah 40 the Lord informs us that He calls each star in the sky by name:

> To whom then will you compare me,
>   that I should be like him? says the Holy One.
> Lift up your eyes on high and see:
>   who created these?
> He who brings out their host by number,
>   calling them all by name,
> by the greatness of his might,
>   and because he is strong in power
>   not one is missing. (vv. 25–26)

The galaxy, of which our solar system is a part, is about 100,000 light-years in diameter. (In case you're a math fanatic, that's about 587,000 trillion miles!) Our galaxy alone has about 100 billion stars. In addition, scientists tell us that our galaxy is one of perhaps as many as a million such galaxies within the optical range of our

most powerful telescopes. This means that there are liter-
ally trillions of stars out there. We bandy about words like
trillion as though we have some idea what they mean.
Have you ever had a trillion dollars? A trillion cents?
Have you ever counted to a trillion, money or not?
Neither have I.

Let's say you decide you would like to try counting to
a trillion. Further, you decide to count just one number
per second. That may seem very slow at first, but by the
time you get to *374,213; 374,214; …*, one number per second may prove too rapid a pace. But for the sake of the
illustration, let's say you could count that fast, one number every second. How long would it take to count to a
trillion? Want to venture a guess? A month? A year? Ten
years? A hundred? Guess again. The answer is more than
thirty thousand years. Thirty thousand years!

God calls each of those trillion-plus stars by name,
and you and I can't even count that high! We have much
too flat a picture of God.

Let me take this a step further. Have you ever had the
opportunity to name a litter of puppies or kittens? (If not,
consider yourself blessed!) If you have, you know the way
most people go about such a project. They look at each
animal, and based on the characteristics of that animal,
they give it a name. Not everyone follows this procedure.
Years ago I had some friends with a German shepherd
named Kitty. I'll be the first to admit that's weird! Most
people, however, look at each animal and offer a name
based on some characteristic of that animal.

Isaiah 40 tells us that God *named* each of those trillion-plus stars. In a hundred lifetimes you and I could
not even come close to *counting* to a trillion, yet the Lord
gave names to more than a trillion stars! We have far too

mundane a perception of what God is really like. However, when we begin to get a clear picture of the greatness of the Lord, our natural reaction is "I want to worship a God like that!"

The God Who Knows Every Thought

Another example of gaining a biblical perspective about God is from Psalm 139. David declares that before he ever speaks a word, God already knows it: "You know when I sit down and when I rise up; you discern my thoughts from afar. You search out my path and my lying down and are acquainted with all my ways. Even before a word is on my tongue, behold, O LORD, you know it altogether" (vv. 2–4).

Have you ever considered the technology involved in cell phones? Radio waves fly through the air and allow us to communicate with one another. Not only can we communicate, but also we can identify the person to whom we are speaking; it sounds like that person. It seemingly makes no difference whether we are in the same room, across town, or across the continent, it still sounds like that person. All from those radio waves whisking through the atmosphere. That's amazing to me!

To that technology add the relatively new advent of call waiting and it becomes even more amazing. You and I can be having a telephone conversation when I get another call. With the push of a button, I put you on hold and I talk with someone else. Your radio waves "stop," the other person's come through, and they don't get mixed up. To me that's astounding! I cannot seem to wrap my brain around that one.

As fantastic as that is, it is an infinitesimally minuscule illustration of what God is like. Have you ever tried to figure out how the Lord can interact with so many people at once? God can clearly and personally speak to you through His Word as you sit reading your Bible during your daily devotion time. At the same time the Lord can hear the heartfelt prayer of repentance from a prostitute in New York City and offer forgiveness. In the exact same moment God can prompt an elderly woman in Jackson Hole, Wyoming, to pray for a missionary in Belarus. At the same time, a native pastor in Guatemala can cry out on behalf of one of his parishioners who has been stricken with a life-threatening disease. God hears and answers them all. All of these situations—and these are just a few—can happen in the exact same moment. Multiply that by millions!

Astonishingly, that's not even the whole story. The real gist of the passage from Psalm 139 I cannot even illustrate. It is too far beyond our comprehension. Yes, the Lord can hear and act on all those prayers at the same time, but *He knows the words even before they are prayed!* All of them. Every word before it is ever on any tongue. All the words before they are on every tongue. God knows each word that will be spoken before it is ever formed in the mouth. Our Lord is far greater than our puny little brains can grasp, and yet catching a glimpse of what God is *really* like causes us to want to worship Him.

God Is Limitless

Our perception of God is much too limited. In holding on to those limited perceptions we do not, as some have said, put God in a box. Instead, we put ourselves in a box. Then one day we find truth from His Word about some aspect of God that we had never before considered, and the box grows. When this happens, we get excited and feel that we now have a handle on what God is really like. However, as long as we think we understand God, we're still in a box. No matter how large your box, it still limits your understanding of a limitless God. This side of heaven we will never plumb the depths of what God is like.

Several places in John's revelation we can see glimpses of heaven. One of the most profound pictures is found in the fourth chapter of the book of Revelation:

> In the center, around the throne, were four living creatures, and they were covered with eyes, in front and in back. The first living creature was like a lion, the second was like an ox, the third had a face like a man, the fourth was like a flying eagle. Each of the four living creatures had six wings and was covered with eyes all around, even under his wings. Day and night they never stop saying: "Holy, holy, holy is the Lord God Almighty, who was, and is, and is to come." (vv. 6–8 NIV)

The four living creatures described here are clearly nothing we have ever seen. They are not earthlings of any type. These beings were most likely created just for heaven. Whatever their precise origin, there is no indication— not even a hint—that they have a fallen nature. Nothing even remotely suggests that they were in need of redemption. Unlike us descendants of Adam, these creatures are holy by nature. Certainly their holiness does not approach the fullness of the holiness of God. However, since they live in heaven, they are apparently sinless creatures. This means that they are holy. These four may be aware of sin, or perhaps they have even seen sin, but they have not experienced it firsthand. They have not been immersed in it as we have. Because of this, they automatically have a purity—a holiness—about them that we have never experienced.

All of this makes their ongoing chanting even more poignant: "Day and night they never stop saying: 'Holy, holy, holy is the Lord God Almighty, who was, and is, and is to come.'" If they, in their holy state, found God so holy that it required them to repeat over and over and over, "Holy, holy, holy...," what will we do when we look upon the holiness of God? We who are fallen by nature, we who have been steeped in sin since birth, what will be our reaction when we gaze upon the holiness of God Almighty?

Too often we lose the sense of reverence for and awe of the Lord. What would happen if, in the middle of a worship service, God came up and tapped you on the shoulder? "I'm here." I'm not talking about just sort of imagining it. In reality, He *is* there. "Where two or three come together in my name, there am I with them" (Matthew 18:20 NIV). Too often we see the people, but we miss Christ. The problem is that we have lost the sense of awe and wonder.

In the Old Testament, God supplied food (manna) for His people in an obviously miraculous fashion. The food was there every morning, with no other possible explanation for this means of sustenance than the hand of God, yet the people took it for granted. We also too often take the presence and actions of the Lord for granted. We need to cultivate a sense of awe and wonder toward God.

Dr. Donald McCullogh wrote a fascinating book entitled *The Trivialization of God*. In it McCullough said this:

> Visit a church on Sunday morning—almost any will do—and you will likely find a congregation comfortably relating to a deity who fits nicely within precise doctrinal positions, or who lends almighty support to social crusades, or who conforms to individual spiritual experiences. But in many churches, you will not likely find much awe or mystery. The only sweaty palms might be those of the preacher unsure whether the sermon will go over; the only shaking knees could be those of the soloist about to sing the offertory.[4]

No wonder our services are so often mundane. We have lost all sense of expectancy. We do not act as though God is really there. If He really did tap us on the shoulder, we would most likely not even notice.

Let's not settle for such a lackadaisical attitude. Instead, ask the Lord to help you recapture—or perhaps find for the first time—a sense of awe toward Him. Search the Scriptures for the real picture of the Lord. Put aside what Josh McDowell calls the "cafeteria eclectic theology" and see the truth of how the Lord portrays Himself in the pages of His Word. In addition, purpose in your heart to not settle for the mundane but to recognize the wonder of God. Cultivate a sense of expectancy in your heart. Recognize anew the holiness of God that caused those already holy creatures to cry out, "Holy, holy, holy is the Lord God Almighty, who was, and is, and is to come."

chapter seven

REVELING IN OUR REDEEMER

*D*o you remember when Jesus healed the man who was born blind? After his healing, the man was called before the Pharisees, who asked him to explain his healing. The man did so, but the Pharisees refused to believe. Finally, the man chided them a bit. "'Never since the world began has it been heard that anyone opened the eyes of a man born blind. If this man were not from God, he could do nothing.' They answered him, 'You were born in utter sin, and would you teach us?' And they cast him out" (John 9:32–34).

The truth is that they were right. He was "born in utter sin." However, so were they. That's the part they didn't recognize. They were so busy admiring their own righteousness that they failed to recognize how truly *un*righteous they were.

Self-righteousness may be the most hideous—most insidious—form of sin there is. We can begin to compare ourselves with others—"I'm not nearly as bad as that person"—and think that God likes us better than those people. How absurd! Apart from God's grace we have nothing. All of our good deeds piled up can never make us righteous in the sight of the Lord. Without His mercy we are helpless and hopelessly lost.

If you honestly want to become a true worshiper, recognizing what God has done for you is imperative. Allow me first to make a concise statement, and then we'll look at the ramifications of the statement. *He has adopted a depraved sinner like you.* Of course, I realize that you might not like the fact that I just called you a depraved sinner, but I am fairly certain that you will get over it.

In his wonderful book *12 Steps for the Recovering Pharisee (Like Me),* John Fischer made this statement: "Our degree of astonishment is related to our personal knowledge of sin. If I have not faced and am not facing the sin in my life, I am not likely to be very impressed with my salvation. It's a nice thing for God to do this for me and all, but I don't really get it."[1]

The apostle Paul said it this way: "For I know that nothing good dwells in me, that is, in my flesh. For I have the desire to do what is right, but not the ability to carry it out. For I do not do the good I want, but the evil I do not want is what I keep on doing" (Romans 7:18–19). Can you relate to that? We know the right things to do; we just don't always do them. In fact, our sinful nature causes us to have a tendency to lean more toward the wrong things than the right ones.

My pastor likens sin to an iceberg. All we can see of an iceberg is the little part that sticks out above the surface of the water. Most of it is hidden below the surface. I have encountered some Christians who have the attitude,

"If I could just get a grip on this one area in my life, I'd probably be a pretty good person." Do you know what would happen if you chopped off the top of an iceberg? More of the iceberg would rise up out of the water.

When it comes to our sin, if the Lord showed us the entire picture, we could not handle it. It's just too ugly. Scripture says, "The heart is deceitful above all things, and desperately sick; who can understand it?" (Jeremiah 17:9). We are far worse than we think.

I find it worthy of note that the apostle Paul spends more than two entire chapters in his letter to the Romans establishing the guilt of the recipients, who are Christ followers. This is not a letter to unbelievers. It is addressed to "the saints." Paul's words are meant to get them (and us) to set aside any possible thoughts of self-righteousness. He builds a very strong case that even they (and we) as believers are guilty and need God's grace.

Even in the Best We Have to Offer

I love the writings of C. S. Lewis. Even his fictional writing carries spiritual weight. In one fictional passage Lewis wrote about two angels looking at a man. "'Look on him, beloved, and love him,' said the first. 'He is indeed but breathing dust and a careless touch would unmake him. And in his best thoughts are such things mingled as, if we thought them, our lights would perish. But he is in the body of [Christ] and his sins are forgiven.'"[2] "In his *best thoughts* are such things mingled as, if we thought them, our lights would perish." What a statement!

Nineteenth-century theologian Archibald Alexander, echoes Lewis's words. "I am deeply convinced that my best duties have fallen far short of the perfection of Thy law, and have been so mingled with sin in the performance, that I might justly be condemned for the most fervent prayer I ever made."[3] "*Justly* be *condemned* for *the most fervent prayer* I ever made." Again, what a statement!

Let me ask you a question. Have you ever been praying publicly, out loud, and afterward thought, "Wow! That was a really good prayer. I wonder if anyone else noticed how good it was." You're smiling, aren't you? I know why, too. Because you can relate. The truth is, you and I are far worse than we realize.

The Bible tells us, "For whoever keeps the whole law but fails in one point has become accountable for all of it" (James 2:10). Just one little misstep, and we're guilty of the whole thing. "Whatever does not proceed from faith is sin" (Romans 14:23b). My guess is that even on good days, before we brush our teeth in the morning, you and I have each accomplished something that "does not proceed from faith."

Unfortunately, sin is a foreign concept in our society today. Too frequently this is true even in the Church. Author and teacher Leonard Sweet made this provocative statement:

> What a wrong journey it has been from "Sinners in the Hands of an Angry God" to "Low-Self-Esteem Clients on the Couch of an Understanding Therapist." Sin is more than self-disesteem and self-victimization. Reformed theologian Cornelius Plantinga puts it like this: Sin has "first and finally a Godward force." This concept is missing in so many discussions where the sinful life has been supplanted by "sickness" or "addiction" or the "unhealthy lifestyle." What's missing is the "Godward force." Sin is an offense against God.[4]

Most of us take sin far too lightly. We must recognize that Leonard Sweet is right. Sin is an offense against God. Those bad attitudes or unkind words are more than just bad attitudes and unkind words. They are sin. Those lustful thoughts are more than just lustful thoughts. They are sin. That seething unforgiveness toward the person who wronged you is sin. That holier-than-thou propensity is *sin*! Sin is what separates us from God. Sin is what sent Jesus to a horrible death on the cross and separation from His Father.

Sovereign Grace Ministries pastor and author C.J. Mahaney wrote these words:

> Let me tell you who I identify with. I identify most with the angry mob screaming, "*Crucify Him!*" That's who we should all identify with. Because apart from God's grace, this is where we would all be standing, and we're only flattering ourselves to think otherwise. Unless you see yourself standing there with the shrieking crowd, full of hostility and hatred for the holy and innocent Lamb of God, you don't really understand the nature and depth of your sin or the necessity of the cross.[5]

Eighteenth-century theologian and revivalist Jonathan Edwards was a profound thinker. Edwards phrased this concept slightly differently.

> When a beggar begs for bread, he pleads the greatness of his poverty and necessity. When a man in distress cries for pity, what more suitable plea can be urged than the extremity of his case?... Those who are not aware of their misery cannot truly look to God for

mercy.... To suppose mercy without supposing misery, or pity without calamity, is a contradiction.[6]

It is not until we recognize how truly heinous our sin is in the sight of God that we can fully embrace His mercy and grace. In his tremendous book *The Discipline of Grace*, Jerry Bridges said, "Your worst days are never so bad that you are beyond the reach of God's grace. And your best days are never so good that you are beyond the need of God's grace."[7]

Let me ask you this: prior to coming into the kingdom of God, how much of the law were we guilty of? The whole thing, of course. Years later, if we have reached the point where there are fewer areas of sin in us, are we any less in need of forgiveness? No! We desperately need His mercy each moment of each day.

The Good News

The good news is that *God has adopted* a depraved sinner like you. "And you were dead in the trespasses and sins" (Ephesians 2:1). Can a dead person make himself alive? Of course not! The Lord grabbed on to you, brought you back to life, and said, "This one is Mine!"

There was an interesting legal quirk in the culture of the New Testament era. As a parent you could disinherit a natural-born child, but you could not disinherit an adopted child. Once you made the decision to adopt a child that was not born into your family, you could no longer reverse that decision. Adoption was a permanent, legal transaction. And it was within that context that the Bible declares, "you have received the Spirit of *adoption* as sons" (Romans 8:15), "we might receive *adoption* as sons"

(Galatians 4:5), and "he predestined us for *adoption* through Jesus Christ, according to the purpose of his will" (Ephesians 1:5). We—you and I—have been adopted by the King! We're His!

Not only has He adopted us, but also He grants us forgiveness and cleansing. "As far as the east is from the west, so far does he remove our transgressions from us" (Psalm 103:12). God's only Son, the Savior, suffered and died for your sins. They're gone!

The message of the gospel has been referred to as an amazing double transfer. Everything that is vile and evil in us is transferred to Jesus, and everything that is good and right in Jesus is transferred to us. He takes our sin, and we stand credited with every righteous thought, word, and deed ever performed by the Lord Jesus while He was here on earth (Isaiah 53:6; Galatians 3:13; Philippians 3:9; Romans 5:18; 2 Corinthians 5:21). If Jesus is your Savior, right now you are holy and righteous before God.

You know, sometimes it seems to me that God has eye problems. Why? Because He doesn't see us as we see ourselves. Actually, it is we who have the eye problems. The Lord's eyesight is far better than ours. God is not bound by physical limitations or small thinking. He sees us as we really are, as He has made us through Christ—holy.

Quite some time ago while I was listening to a Christian radio talk show, a young woman called in and asked a couple of seemingly mundane questions. The host realized that the woman was skirting the issue for which she really called and directly asked her what her real question was. The woman began to cry. Through sobs and strained voice she confided that some Christian friends had told her that she had committed the unpardonable sin, blaspheming the Holy Spirit (see Mark

3:29), and that she could no longer be saved. She wanted to know what to do.

The talk show host handled it perfectly. I didn't write down his exact words, but in essence he said this: "You did not commit the unpardonable sin. Please hear what I am saying to you. I am not saying, 'I don't think you did' or 'You probably did not.' I am telling you without any wavering or doubting that you did not commit the unpardonable sin. I can say that, even without knowing the details of what you've done, because I can hear your repentance. If you had committed the unforgivable sin, your heart would be completely hard. You would have no regret. You would be cold and hard and calloused, but you're not. You are very obviously sincerely sorry for whatever it is that you have done. With that kind of heart attitude, God will always take you back and offer forgiveness."

He is exactly right. As long as there is repentance, as long as there is a sincere turning to God, there will *always* be forgiveness.

Yes, I know there are those who "deliberately keep on sinning" and have "trampled the Son of God under foot" and "insulted the Spirit of grace" (Hebrews 10:26, 29 NIV). My experience, though, has been that those people are rare in the Church. Most people loathe their sins. Their attitude is like that of the apostle Paul. "For I do not do the good I want, but the evil I do not want is what I keep on doing" (Romans 7:19). As long as the heart is longing for God, as long as the Holy Spirit is bringing conviction, as long as we are walking in honest repentance before the Lord, there will always be forgiveness.

Please understand that sin may very well have ongoing consequences. The temporal results of our wrongdoings may not be altered by our repenting. However, even in the midst of those consequences, God still loves the sinner intensely. The Lord declares, "I have loved you with an everlasting love" (Jeremiah 31:3).

The Pivotal Point

Let me try this from a different angle. Ask any Jew, "What is the pivotal point of all of history?" If they really know and understand their history, all Jews would give the same answer: the Exodus. This was, after all, a phenomenal miracle of mind-boggling proportions. Only God could have caused such a series of events to take place.

The Exodus began with the plagues, horrific, nightmarish events that left the nation of Egypt in turmoil. Think about it. Water turned to blood. In a culture that worshiped the Nile River, water was more than a thirst quencher. Then came the frogs. Everywhere. Okay, the Egyptians' homes were not as tightly built as homes in our society, but I somehow don't think the Egyptians even liked the idea of frogs in their kitchens, their beds, their food, and their clothes. It must have been awful. But it got worse. The frogs all died, and the stench of their decaying, rotting carcasses was almost unbearable. Then, just as the people began to get accustomed to the smell, along came gnats and then flies. Not just a nice little group, but storm-cloud-size swarms. Maybe the people couldn't see their sister-in-law's house down the road because of the thickness of the raging insects. Perhaps while calling to their children, they swallowed a mouthful of the flying creatures. They probably hoped, "This can't continue much longer, can it?" But it did.

Next was pestilence. Disease wiped out the Egyptian cattle in the fields. Then boils covered the Egyptians.

Webster's defines a boil as "an inflamed, painful, pus-filled swelling on the skin." All over their bodies?! No thanks. Still the plagues continued. Hail wiped out a significant portion of the Egyptian crops and much of the remaining livestock. Any crops and trees that had survived were then devoured by an invading army of swarming locusts. Next, thick, palpable darkness covered the Egyptians, who could see nothing. Total blackness engulfed their lives. Then, finally, when they thought nothing could be any worse, the firstborn of each Egyptian family died. Their people, their nation, was devastated and ravaged.

As a result, the Israelites were sent packing. They left Egypt with Pharaoh's permission, but his consent was short-lived. Pharaoh quickly changed his mind and pursued the Hebrew people.

Guided by God's hand, Moses and the Israelites camped at the Red Sea. This seemed to be a foolish tactical error. They had no escape route. They were trapped. The Egyptian army was on one side of them, and the Red Sea on the other. The Israelites had no way out. Well, almost no way out…

God split the sea open. A touch of His hand, a breath from His mouth, and the water swept aside. Instead of the wet, swamplike bottom of the seabed, there was dry ground, solid enough for the Israelites to walk on. There was no way out, but God made a way.

The nation of Israel walked across to the other side, snatched out of the hands of their enemy by their benevolent Creator. When the enemy tried to pursue them, the Lord released the waters and the adversaries were annihilated, drowned in the foaming waters of the sea. The most powerful army on the face of the earth was wiped out through one quick action by the Lord.

This entire series of events—the Exodus of the Jewish people from Egypt—is a miracle that could come only from the hand of the Almighty. Our most vivid dreams—or nightmares—could not conjure up such a scenario. Only God could have caused such a miracle. That's why Jews would refer to this as the major event of their history. From the Jewish perspective, nothing has ever happened that compares with this colossal rescue.

As believers in Jesus, we know better. The true pivotal point of history is the cross, a rescue of even more monumental proportions. People destined for hell were granted a full and complete pardon. The holy, sinless Son of God died an excruciating death to pay the ransom for sinners like you and me. Rebellious and stiff-necked people were lovingly snatched out of the hands of the enemy by their benevolent Creator.

The Exodus was the foreshadowing. The cross was the real event. As the hole that my wife just dug in her garden for a tomato plant compares to the Grand Canyon, so does the Exodus compare to the cross. There is no real comparison. What the Lord has done for us is beyond all human comprehension.

Most of the book of Deuteronomy is a monologue. God told Moses that he, Moses, would not be going into the Promised Land. Moses was about to die. So he spoke to the people, offering his final words of encouragement and exhortation. It was his farewell address to those who were preparing to take possession of the Promised Land.

Moses' words cover a variety of topics. The man who had led these people for the past forty years undoubtedly had much on his mind to tell them. After all, his final words would hopefully be what they would remember most. Like a father about to depart from his children,

Moses had so many things he wanted to say. Although he apparently talked for quite a while, and the topics were indeed broad ranging, his message contained a clear and obvious recurring theme: Remember the Lord's mercy to you. Don't ever forget that you were slaves and He rescued you. Always remember what you have seen God do. Over and over again throughout the speech, Moses repeatedly told the people to call to mind how the Lord had intervened on their behalf.

In similar manner, the writers of the New Testament keep pointing us to the cross. Again and again we are admonished to remember Jesus and His death on Calvary. The intervention of our merciful Redeemer is paramount. It is far more amazing than the Exodus story. It is the pivotal point of all of human history. We must keep calling to mind what God has done for us.

The Making of a Covenant

If you are at all familiar with the Old Testament, you probably recall how people would make covenants with each other. The two parties making the covenant would agree together about whatever their covenant would be. They then would take various animals—some of the common ones were heifers, goats, and rams—and slaughter them. Now hang on, because this is going to get a little bit gory. Bear with me, though, because the end will be worthwhile.

The parties to the covenant would then cut the animals in half. The animals were sliced right down the middle. Nothing was removed. Quite a lot of the blood obviously ran out, but the entrails and all were still in the animals. The halves of those creatures would then be laid out in two rows, with a space between the rows just wide enough for the two parties to fit. Then the covenant makers would walk between the halves of those slaughtered animals.

The significance of this symbolism is lost in our culture. We don't generally perform ceremonies like this in our society. However, in that culture, the meaning was obvious. By performing such an observance, the two parties were saying, "If I ever break this covenant, may what happened to these animals happen to me." It was a deadly serious ritual, with powerful significance.

As you consider the meaning, keep in mind that this was the same type of covenant that God made with Abraham in Genesis 15:9–21. The Lord told Abraham to get the animals, kill them, and cut them in half. Abraham did exactly as he was instructed. What happened next, though, is amazing to me. God caused Abraham to fall into a deep sleep, and the Lord went between the animal halves alone. While Abraham was unconscious, the Lord traversed the space unaccompanied between those cut-in-two animals. In essence, what God was saying by His actions was, "If *either* of us ever breaks this covenant, may what happened to these animals happen to Me." And that, my friend, is exactly what Jesus did for us on the cross. He took the punishment that you and I deserved and gave us mercy and forgiveness.

In his excellent book *Christ Our Mediator*, C.J. Mahaney talks about Jesus' praying, "Let this cup pass from Me." He points out that Christ is referring not to a literal cup but to the cup of God's wrath for your sins and mine.

As we watch Jesus pray in agony in Gethsemane, He has every right to turn His tearful eyes toward you and me and shout, "This is *your* cup. *You're* responsible for this. It's *your* sin! *You* drink it." This cup should rightfully be thrust into my hand and yours.

Instead, Jesus freely takes it Himself…so that from the cross He can look down at you and me, whisper our names and say, "I drain this cup for you—for you who have lived in defiance of Me, who have hated Me, who have opposed Me. I drink it all…for *you*."[8]

This is why Paul could write to the believers in Rome with such total confidence, "There is therefore now no condemnation for those who are in Christ Jesus. For the law of the Spirit of life has set you free in Christ Jesus from the law of sin and death" (Romans 8:1–2).

Paul concludes that same chapter with these words: "For I am convinced that neither death nor life, neither angels nor demons, neither the present nor the future, nor any powers, neither height nor depth, nor anything else in all creation, will be able to separate us from the love of God that is in Christ Jesus our Lord" (Romans 8:38–39 NIV). Death, life, angels, demons, present, future, powers, height, depth, anything in all creation. Wow! That's an all-inclusive list. None of those things can separate us from the love of God.

One Leper Returning

So what does all this mean for us as worshipers? The great reformer Martin Luther once described worship as one leper returning. Do you remember the ten lepers that Jesus healed? (See Luke 17:11–19.) Only one returned to Jesus and said, "Thank You." We who have been healed from something far worse than a physical disease like leprosy should be ever thankful for what the Lord has done for us. We who were destined for eternity in hell now have been granted a full pardon and a paid-in-full ticket for heaven. Could anything be more wonderful? Does not the simple recognition of that fact stir within you a desire to worship the Lord right now?

In his book *Worship 101*, Andrew G. Robbins asks a provocative question: "Why are Christians not inspired to worship?"[9] Further along, he says, "When you think of what our Savior has saved us from, the apathy in most churches is truly sickening."[10] Earlier he states, "Many of our churches are filled with people who are not inspired to do much more than emotionlessly sing along with the songs because they do not have a concept of God's Law and therefore have a shallow appreciation of His grace."[11] Robbins is accurate in his assessment. If we truly understand what the Lord has done, how can we not worship?

Canadian pastor and author Mark Buchanan has an amazing gift of words. In his book *Your God Is Too Safe*, Buchanan offered these thoughts:

I don't know why, but I know that virtue has weak, straggling roots, and vice has wild, racing ones. Virtue withers as quickly as plucked grass, spreads as slowly as lichen. But vice—ah, vice flourishes like the weeds.

I know that the most captivating, staggering, extravagant fact in all time and space—that God came down, became one of us, died by us and died for us, did it to make us His children and bride, and now walks every moment with us in love and companionship—that this amazing truth I can treat as no more important than, and forget as easily as, my yearly car insurance renewal. It can become dull routine, one more thing to know, do, worry about. One more thing to try to remember.

Such a God doing such a thing surpasses all things in greatness and marvel. Nothing even remotely, even vaguely, compares with it. Yet the Sunday flyers, with yet another 40 percent off sale on kitchenware at Wal-Mart, or the pages with reviews of the latest batch of books or movies, can distract me from it. A simple backache can ruin my joy in it. An unexpected car expense can steal away my thankfulness for it.[12]

The Lord of all creation reached down and rescued you. You were on a direct path—do not pass GO, do not collect anything—to hell, when the benevolent Creator redeemed you. In one of his songs, Rich Mullins calls the love of God a "reckless, raging fury." That's a powerful—and accurate—description. Will you allow the truth of His mercy and grace to cause you to become a true worshiper of His?

If we really want to be true worshipers, we need to regularly be reminded—and to remind ourselves—of what God has done for us. As Luther suggests, we should be like that one leper returning to thank the Lord. We have been rescued and redeemed by the greatest act of love in history. We have been adopted as God's children. With grateful hearts let us worship our loving Father.

chapter eight

CONCLUSION

*T*he book of Psalms is divided into five books or sections. The first section includes chapters 1 through 41. The next is 42 through 72. The third section comprises 73 through 89. Chapters 90 through 106 make up the fourth. The last section includes chapters 107 through 150. Most Bibles show this delineation, referring to the sections as "Book One," "Book Two," and so on.

Throughout the entire book of Psalms we see the full gamut of human emotion depicted. There is rejoicing and sorrow, exaltation and lament. It's all there. The very highest points of our earthly experience and the lowest are all mixed in together.

Interestingly, each section (or book) in Psalms ends in nearly identical fashion: with words of praise for the God of Israel. Take a look at the endings of each section:

Blessed be the LORD, the God of Israel, from everlasting to everlasting! Amen and Amen. (Psalm 41:13)

Blessed be the LORD, the God of Israel, who alone does wondrous things. Blessed be his glorious name forever; may the whole earth be filled with his glory! Amen and Amen! (Psalm 72:18–19)

Blessed be the LORD forever! Amen and Amen. (Psalm 89:52)

Blessed be the LORD, the God of Israel, from everlasting to everlasting! And let all the people say, "Amen!" Praise the LORD! (Psalm 106:48)

Praise the LORD! Praise God in his sanctuary; praise him in his mighty heavens! Praise him for his mighty deeds; praise him according to his excellent greatness! Praise him with trumpet sound; praise him with lute and harp! Praise him with tambourine and dance; praise him with strings and pipe! Praise him with sounding cymbals; praise him with loud clashing cymbals! Let everything that has breath praise the LORD! Praise the LORD! (Psalm 150)

Regardless of what has come before—sadness or gladness, dancing or mourning—the ending point is the same: praise to the Lord!

Worship is not meant to be just some ethereal experience. I have met people who go from one worship service to the next, even one worship conference to the next, looking for their next "worship experience." Truthfully, there is little difference between those people and the drug addict looking for his next fix.

Scripture tells us, "Do not be conformed to this world, but be transformed by the renewal of your mind" (Romans 12:2). Changing how we think will change our actions. In the context of worship, then, truly *understanding* worship from a biblical perspective will alter *how* we worship.

In this book we have not discussed mystical experiences of worship. Instead we have explored the truth of God's Word about worship. We have learned much about what Jesus meant when He told the Samaritan woman at the well that "true worshipers will worship the Father in spirit and truth" (John 4:23). In his book *Exploring Worship*, one of the very first books to address the issue of worship in modern society, Bob Sorge said this:

> When Jesus spoke of worshiping in truth, he meant that worship must involve the mind. Worship that involves only the spirit is insufficient; the mind must also be exerted. Some people wait for a floaty, ethereal feeling to come over them before they are sure they have really worshiped. They fail to realize that worship involves all of one's mental faculties and is experienced at the height of mental awareness. The more we exert our minds in worship, the more meaningful our worship is likely to be.[1]

The more you exert your mind, as Sorge says, and truly understand what worship is, who God is, and what He has done for you, the more you will become a true worshiper.

Worship is not about having an eerie, spiritual experience. It is a commitment to have your heart turned toward God. My pastor said it this way:

Worship, as the Revelation describes it, is grand, imposing, breathtaking, but it is also simple, even repetitious. Worshiping God does not require an ongoing procession of novelty. A heart cleansed by the blood and a life submitted to Him, expressing themselves fervently to glorify Him, are quite enough![2]

Let me close with a wonderful quotation by Manfred Koehler from an article he wrote, entitled "What Will I Do with a Crown?"

Consider Christian's story in John Bunyan's *The Pilgrim's Progress*. Christian has long since dropped the burden of his sin at the cross, has faithfully finished his journey, and has recently crossed the River of Death. As he approaches the King, his back is now laden with another burden, a large hemp sack crammed full of heavy objects. Christian bends under the weight of his load, but his shining face shows no strain.

With a smile, he drops the overflowing bag at Jesus' feet. Several silver coins tumble to the floor, rolling until they strike the great throne. Reaching inside, Christian pulls out a large gold ingot that gleams white in the brilliance of the King's presence. Gently caressing the gold bar, he stoops and lays it on the floor, his eyes brimming as he gazes at his Savior. "Thank you," Christian whispers. The heads of the watching hosts tilt in murmured agreement.

Reaching in again, he pulls out a diamond the size of his fist. It sparkles with the light of a hundred stars. Cupping it in both hands, Christian bows and gently rests the precious stone between the nail-scarred feet.

"I love you," Christian mouths, his whisper ringing through the halls of heaven.

The faithful believer rises, pulling out the next item with great care. The emerging crown is huge, glittering in prisms of unearthly color. Seraphim hold their breath in awe. He sinks to his knees, the crown extended with trembling hands.

"You are worthy," Christian cries, his voice breaking with emotion. The hosts kneel with him.

And the humble hemp sack is still nine-tenths full.[3]

May you and I be found in the same posture as Christian, with our eyes turned toward the Redeemer-Creator, our hearts full of love and adoration for Him alone.

FURTHER THOUGHTS TO INSPIRE WORSHIP

As you can see from the numerous authors I've quoted throughout this book, many books have already been published on the subject of worship. Some are obviously better than others, but most have at least something of value to offer the reader.

What follows is a collection of additional quotable quotes I've gleaned from my reading over the years. These quotes didn't seem to fit in a specific section of this book, but I find them thought provoking. I hope they challenge and inspire you as much as they have me.

Jim Cymbala

If we don't want to experience God's closeness here on earth, why would we want to go to heaven anyway? He is the center of everything there. If we don't enjoy being in his presence here and now, then heaven would not be heaven for us. Why would he send anyone there who doesn't long for him passionately here on earth?[1]

Jack Hayford

One of our members, with the best of motives, once suggested, "Pastor, if you didn't teach and invite people to lift their hands in worship, I think our church would grow faster," and then added, "I think you might injure some people's pride."

"Injure pride?" I said gently. "Why, I was hoping to kill it altogether."[2]

John Wesley wrote a preface to a songbook, *Sacred Melody,* published in 1761. In it he gave several admonitions to those who would engage in singing the songs contained in the book. Included were these words:

> Sing lustily and with good courage. Beware of singing as if you were half dead, or half asleep; but lift your voice with strength.... Sing modestly. Do not bawl, so as to be heard above or distinct from the rest of the congregation, that you may not destroy the harmony; but strive to unite your voices together, so as to make one clear melodious sound.... Above all sing spiritually. Have an eye to God in every word you sing. Aim at pleasing him more than yourself, or any other creature. In order to do this attend strictly to the sense of what you sing, and see that your heart is not carried away with the sound, but offered to God continually; so shall your singing be such as the Lord will approve here, and reward you when he cometh in the clouds of heaven.[3]

N. T. Wright

> The great multitude in Revelation which no man can number aren't playing cricket. They aren't going shopping. They are *worshipping*. Sounds boring? If so, it shows how impoverished our idea of worship has become.[4]

Ernest B. Gentile

> God did not inspire His writers to record in detail the order of church meetings because He knew man's tendency to stylize, formalize and institutionalize worship.... Worship in the universal church of Christ certainly has common elements, but the diversity of cultures, races, languages, and experiences demands variety of expression.... God has given stable components for worship services to be expressed through flexible forms.[5]

David Peterson

> Fundamentally, then, worship in the New Testament means believing the gospel and responding with one's whole life and being to the person and work of God's Son, in the power of the Holy Spirit.[6]

N. T. Wright

> We in the modern West have forgotten *how* to celebrate, probably because we've forgotten *why*. Large meals, lots of drink, and behaving childishly is a parody of true celebration; but it's what you might expect when we forget that our maker is also our lover. That was the condition of Israel in exile, the people addressed in Isaiah 35. Israel was called to be the people of God, but in exile it had all gone stale. People in our society know in their bones that they are made to reflect God's image; but they feel exiled, futile, and stale; so they go in for tired and shoddy celebration, seen only too clearly in the forced frivolity of television programmes over Christmas and

New Year. Contrast that mood with the one Isaiah held out to the exiles:

> The wilderness and the dry land shall be glad,
> the desert shall rejoice and blossom;
> like the crocus it shall blossom abundantly,
> and rejoice with joy and singing...
> They shall see the glory of the LORD,
> the majesty of our God.
> ...the ransomed of the LORD shall return,
> and come to Zion with singing;
> everlasting joy shall be upon their heads;
> they shall obtain joy and gladness,
> and sorrow and sighing shall flee away.

When we realize once again that our God is the one who loves us into new life, then we will really know how to celebrate.[7]

Buddy Owens

Worship is an act of humility. It is impossible to truly worship and be proud at the same time, because worship is a declaration of dependence—it is an honest admission that God is greater than I am.[8]

Janet Lindeblad Janzen with *Richard Foster*

Worship is productive. It is meaningful work. Under David's leadership it became a full-time job for some of the priests "to invoke, to thank and to praise the LORD" (1 Chronicles 16:4). You and I are now part of that priesthood, the priesthood of all believers. The ministry of worship has become our vocation, our calling as well.[9]

Notes

Introduction

1. Tricia McCary Rhodes, "Created for Delight," in *Discipleship Journal*, November/December 2002.

Chapter 1

1. Malapropism is a ludicrous misuse of a word.
2. W. Nicholls, *Jacob's Ladder: The Meaning of Worship, Ecumenical Studies in Worship No. 4* (London: Lutterworth, 1958), 9.
3. Vernon M. Whaley, Ph.D., *Understanding Music & Worship in the Local Church* (Wheaton, Ill.: Evangelical Training Association, 1995), 15.
4. Pastor Nick Ittzes, Christian Outreach Church, Hillsboro, Missouri, Sunday sermon, April 25, 2004.
5. N. T. Wright, *For All God's Worth* (Grand Rapids: William B. Eerdmans Publishing Company, 1997), 9.
6. Jerry Bridges, *The Joy of Fearing God* (Colorado Springs: WaterBrook Press, 1997), 247.

Chapter 2

1. Pastor Nick Ittzes, Christian Outreach Church, Hillsboro, Missouri, Sunday sermon, April 25, 2004.
2. Puritan Stephen Charnock, quoted by Jerry Bridges in *I Exalt You, O God* (Colorado Springs: WaterBrook Press, 2001).

3. Special thanks to Pastor Jerry Worsham of Grace Church in Racine, Wisconsin, for these insights.

Chapter 3

1. Anne Ortlund, *Up with Worship* (Glendale, Calif.: Regal Books, 1975), 64.
2. The KJV lists the term *organ* three times as a musical instrument, but newer translations use the word as a wind instrument.

Chapter 5

1. Mark Buchanan, *Your God Is Too Safe* (Sisters, Ore.: Multnomah Publishers, 2001), 174.
2. Ronald B. Allen and Gordon L. Borror, *Worship: Rediscovering the Missing Jewel* (Portland, Ore.: Multnomah Publishers, 1982), 24.

Chapter 6

1. De Mello, quoted in Brennan Manning, *The Ragamuffin Gospel* (Sisters, Ore.: Multnomah Publishers, 2000), 199–200.
2. Robert W. Bailey, *New Ways in Christian Worship* (Nashville: Broadman, 1981).
3. Josh McDowell, quoted in an e-mail from Penny Woods, Josh McDowell Ministry, October 4, 2004.
4. Donald W. McCullogh, *The Trivialization of God* (Colorado Springs: NavPress, 1995).

Chapter 7

1. John Fischer, *12 Steps for the Recovering Pharisee (Like Me)* (Minneapolis: Bethany House Publishers, 2000), 138.
2. C. S. Lewis, *Perelandra* (New York: The Macmillan Company, 1944), 195.

3. Quoted in Jerry Bridges, *I Exalt You, O God* (Colorado Springs: WaterBrook Press, 2001).

4. Leonard Sweet, *Out of the Question (Into the Mystery)* (Colorado Springs: WaterBrook Press, 2004), 144.

5. C.J. Mahaney, *Christ Our Mediator* (Sisters, Ore.: Multnomah Publishers, 2004), 65–66.

6. Jonathan Edwards, "I Beg Your Pardon," in *Discipleship Journal*, November/December 2005.

7. Jerry Bridges, *The Discipline of Grace* (Colorado Springs: NavPress, 1994), 18.

8. Mahaney, *Christ Our Mediator*, 57–58.

9. Andrew G. Robbins, *Worship 101* (Bloomington, Ind.: AuthorHouse, 2004), 22.

10. Ibid., 24.

11. Ibid., 10.

12. Mark Buchanan, *Your God Is Too Safe* (Sisters, Ore.: Multnomah Publishers, 2001), 143–144.

Chapter 8

1. Bob Sorge, *Exploring Worship* (Canandaigua, N.Y.: Bob Sorge, 1987), 80.

2. Pastor Nick Ittzes, Christian Outreach Church, Hillsboro, Missouri, Sunday sermon, April 25, 2004.

3. Manfred Koehler, "What Will I Do with a Crown?" *Discipleship Journal*, September/October 2002.

Further Thoughts to Inspire Worship

1. Jim Cymbala, *Fresh Wind, Fresh Fire* (Grand Rapids: Zondervan Publishing House, 1997), 58–59.

2. Jack Hayford, "How God Evaluates Worship," Internet article, http://www.JackHayford.com.

3. From John Wesley's preface to *Sacred Melody*, 1761, quoted in *The United Methodist Hymnal* (Nashville: Abingdon Press, 1989), vii.

4. N. T. Wright, *For All God's Worth* (Grand Rapids: William B. Eerdmans Publishing Company, 1997), 7.

5. Ernest B. Gentile, *Worship God!* (Portland, Ore.: Bible Temple Publishing, 1994), 34–35.

6. David Peterson, *Engaging with God* (Downers Grove, Ill.: InterVarsity Press, 1992), 286.

7. Wright, *For All God's Worth*, 15–16.

8. Buddy Owens, *The Way of a Worshiper* (San Clemente, Calif.: Maranatha! Publishing, 2002), 49.

9. Janet Lindeblad Janzen with Richard Foster, *Songs for Renewal* (New York: HarperCollins Publishers, 1995), 65.